HIGHWAYS OF BRITAIN

THEN AND NOW

*Dedicated to the memory of Margaret Ann Powell, my soulmate, 1950-2015.
I miss you love.*

HIGHWAYS OF BRITAIN
THEN AND NOW

CHRIS 'WOLFIE' COOPER

An Imprint of Pen & Sword Books Ltd

HIGHWAYS OF BRITAIN – THEN AND NOW
© After the Battle and Chris 'Wolfie' Cooper, 2025

Published by After the Battle
An imprint of Pen & Sword Books Ltd
George House, Units 12 & 13, Beevor Street, Off Pontefract Road,
Barnsley, South Yorkshire, S71 1HN, England
Tel. 01226 734222
Fax. 01226 734438
Email: enquiries@pen-and-sword.co.uk
Website: **www.afterthebattle.com**
www.pen-and-sword.co.uk

Printed and bound in India by Parksons Graphics Pvt. Ltd.

ISBN: 9781036126735

Commissioning Editor: Rob Green
Author: Chris 'Wolfie' Cooper
Design: SJmagic DESIGN SERVICES, India
Cover Design: Jon Wilkinson

Acknowledgements:
In the writing of this book, I was assisted by Google Earth which is a brilliant resource for looking around the country from your desk. Also, many Facebook groups with old photos in which helped me to orientate myself on more than one occasion. SABRE is a great resource for information either in the main forums or the 'Roaders Digest' a Wiki full of information as well as the old maps sections. Lastly the National Library of Scotland's map resource section which was of great assistance in plotting the courses of the old roads.

Photo Credit Abbreviations:
GEP – Google Earth Pro   CC – Chris Cooper   PC - postcard

Front Cover:
The garage at Ferrybridge on the Great North Road. When the dual carriageway was built on an embankment it obliterated this section of road. The only clue is the old schoolhouse on the right. (unknown and GEP)

Half title page:
This is a fork on a back road in North Yorkshire. You can clearly see that one arm has been upgraded to a surfaced road and the other has not. It gives us a good indication of what most roads would have looked like right up until the 20th century.

Back Cover:
Top: The Old Fox inn on the Great North Road is still there as a truck stop, if a little less glamorous than it once was. (PC and GEP)

Centre: The Scarborough mail coach in the Market Place at Malton, North Yorkshire. (Unknown and CC)

Bottom: The Great North Road in Colsterworth, Lincolnshire (PC and GEP)

CONTENTS

Introduction 6

The Pre-Roman Era 11

Roman and Medieval Roads 19

Changes 1500 – 1700 35

Turnpiking and the Coaching Era 48

The Fall and Rise of Roads and Modern Times 75

Street Furniture, Alterations and other Interesting Things 90

INTRODUCTION

WHEN I WROTE ABOUT the Great North Road, little did I know I was setting myself up with a whole load of problems. After my voyage of discovery sniffing out all the various alterations, I now find myself not being able to ride around the country without seeing similar alterations wherever I go. Cut off stubs, ox-bow lay-bys, orphaned bits of road, altered junctions, the list goes on. It got

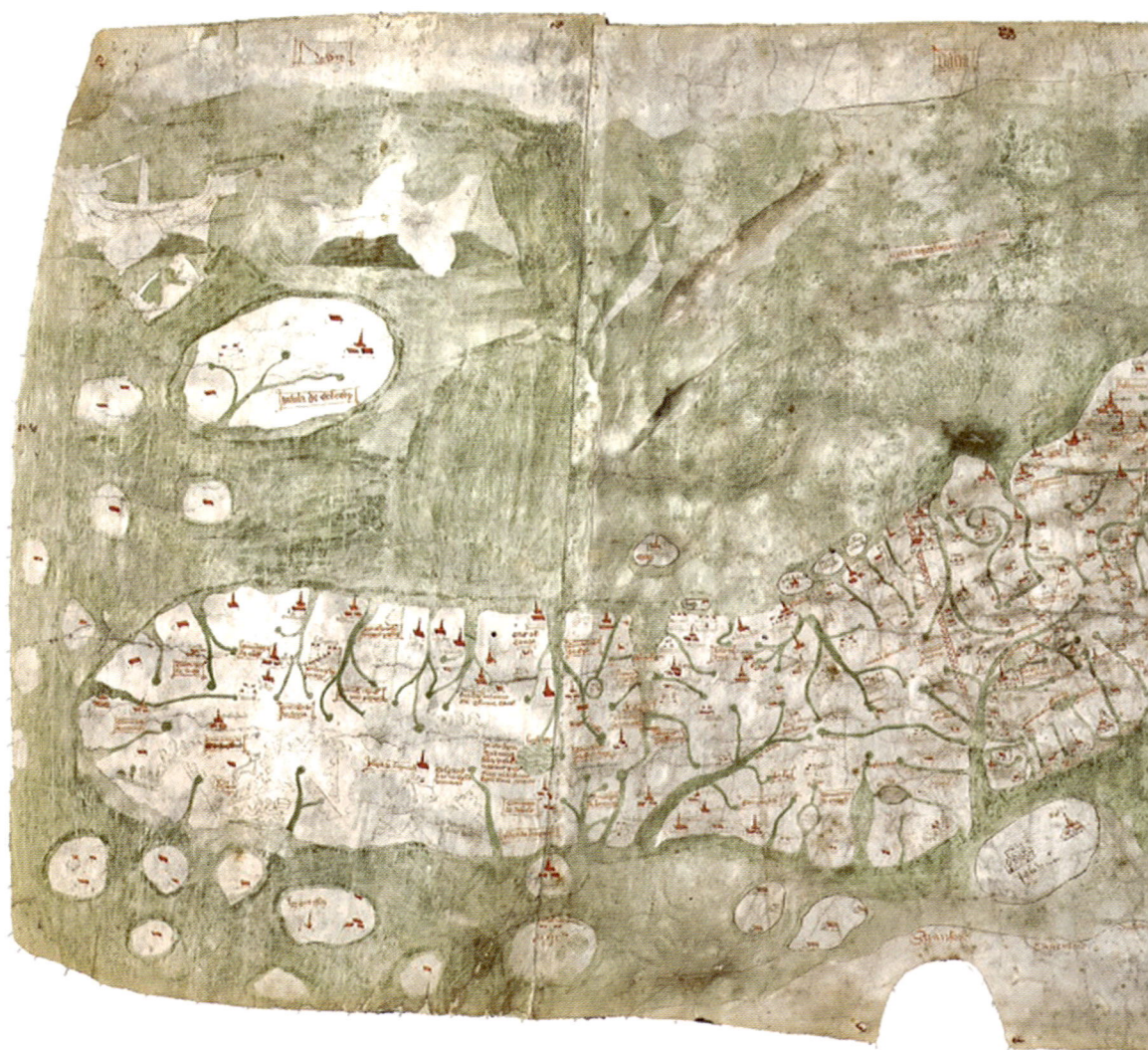

me wondering, how did it all happen? Where did it all start? And so, another book is born.

I stated in the first chapter of my previous book that historically there was not much requirement for a dedicated road system prior to the Roman invasion. I am not so sure about that now; the road system may not have been planned but it was there. I read quite a lot of history, particularly military history, and I have an interest in military operations of earlier eras. There was trade certainly by the Neolithic period. All these armies chasing around Britain must have known where they were going! The Saxon and Viking invasions for instance. There is clear evidence that Kings and armies moved extensively around the country. There were distinct kingdoms in

The Gough map of Great Britain. The original source of this map is unknown and it is believed to date from the late 14th century. It is the first known map to show roads although sources differ as to how accurate they are and the distances are measured in an unknown unit.

Britain by the 8th century, Northumberland, Mercia, Wessex, East Anglia, etc. There must have been communication between them, messengers, state visits and so on. Many of the rulers were related by marriage or otherwise. The movements of the Kings are known in some cases as places where they celebrated Easter or Christmas are recorded, and these places are situated all over the country.

Now I do not expect that there were many signposts around in those days so I can only make the assumption that there were people who knew where they were going. Perhaps they were like pilots in shipping. Each port has someone who knows the port extensively and can guide ships in because the ship's crew are not familiar with the port. Maybe each area had its experts, the men who travelled locally and who knew the pathways in their area. Perhaps travellers were passed on from one area to the next or were there those who travelled further afield? Was there a prehistoric equivalent of us, the lorry driver, someone that knew his way around the whole country? I suspect not, it would have taken someone years and years in those times to learn their way around only having the horse or foot for transport. It is quite feasible of course that there were folk familiar with a long-distance route that they used regularly, for instance, cattle drovers who went from Wales to London every year.

A NOTE ON SABRE, ROAD TERMINOLOGY AND TRUCKNET

You may, or then again may not, be surprised to find out that you are not the only one with a healthy interest in roads. I believe a calendar consisting of photographs of roundabouts in the West Midlands was a best seller one Christmas. It may help to know that you are not alone, that many more folk than you might think share your interest. In fact, there is a thriving web community of so called 'roadgeeks', although the engineers and truck drivers and planners and all the others who inhabit that community might not really be geeks any more than you are. May I introduce you to SABRE. The Society for All British Road Enthusiasts. www.sabre-roads.org.uk

This is a very comprehensive site dedicated to Britain's roads and if you cannot find the information you want on SABRE or any of the affiliated websites, then there is a thriving forum in which you will find experts on everything from the old London ringways plan to the disappearing road at Mam Tor. There are links to many other websites where you will find all sorts of fascinating facts, and an ever-growing project to catalogue every single one of Britain's numbered roads. Certainly, I have used their collective knowledge on many occasions.

It is necessary to have a certain amount of terminology when discussing a subject and roads are no exception. I have tried to keep it to a bare minimum but a couple of terms need explanation. I have used the terms generally used within SABRE, which as far as I am aware are in use amongst the planning engineers too. A road generally has a letter/number designation where the letter indicates how many carriageways, and the number how many lanes per carriageway. Your standard single carriageway road is an S2 road. If it has a 'suicide lane' up the middle it becomes S3. If a central reservation splits the road into dual carriageway, then it becomes a D2. So, a motorway with 3 lanes each way is a D3, occasionally with an M added to show special (motorway) status e.g. D3M. There are derivatives of these, but you will not really need to understand any more than S2, S3, D2, and D3.

The other terms I will use are GSJ and 'multiplex'. GSJ stands for Grade Separated Junction. A GSJ is a junction where slip roads or bridges exist so that traffic entering or leaving a road does not need to cross the opposing carriageway to do so. For example, a right turn across a dual carriageway *is not* a GSJ, but leaving via a slip road on your own side, then crossing under or over the dual carriageway via a tunnel or bridge *is* a GSJ. In general, a fast free flowing road with GSJs is far safer than one without. Junctions not GSJ'd are known as 'at-grade'.

A multiplex is where two different road numbers share the same actual road. Imagine a hypothetical crossroads where the A1234 and the A5678 meet and cross. The road-space in the centre of the crossroads is in fact shared by both roads. Now extend that to the A5678 joining the A1234 at a T junction and then leaving it at another T junction half a mile up the road. The half mile between the two T junctions is a multiplex. They can be much longer than half a mile. (Please note that the two roads do not in reality meet, in fact the A5678 does not even exist!). As a road in Britain can only have one number, one is considered 'dominant' and so the other would normally be given in brackets on a sign. So, the above half mile would be numbered A1234 (A5678). A good example is the M62 north of Manchester where it multiplexes with the M60 Manchester orbital for some distance. The term 'multiplex' is not believed to be the official term, if there is one!

For those of you like me who work in the road haulage sector, there is an internet forum where current and ex lorry drivers chat and reminisce. I picked their brains more than once in the writing of this and earlier books. If you are interested to visit the forum it can be found at www.trucknetuk.com.

This engraving shows a busy Bayswater turnpike in west London.

This is the same spot today. No sheep wandering around now. (GEP)

    I should mention that I am not a historian, I am simply a well-read wagon driver. Some of what I write is bound to be conjecture but where this occurs, I will make this clear in the text.

Chris Cooper
Ryedale, North Yorkshire
gnrauthor@gmail.com
2016-2024

THE PRE-ROMAN ERA

THE BASIC UNIT OF communal human settlement in Britain is the parish. It is the lowest level of local government and developed from the manorial feudal system being later taken over by the church. There was a split in the 19th century that gave rise to civil parishes for local government as opposed to the religious ones.

I am guessing that the parish is probably based on the small family unit. In the Iron age (circa 800BC to the Roman conquest) Britain was populated by tribes of either Celtic or Pict origins. These tribes were farmers and each family unit would have had some land with which to feed themselves and provide surplus for sale or tithe. The family units were probably quite extensive including several generations plus artisans and slaves and other workers and would have been spread over a collection of dwellings. In each area there were a number of such units and a larger central place where the leaders lived and people met up for markets or fairs. These places grew into the villages and market towns that are familiar in our rural areas today.

So, to the burning question, how did they get around between these places? Well, as a rule, they walked or rode. You would have the path from your house to the other houses or fields in your settlement and then a path to the neighbouring settlements and another path to the nearest market town. Of course, the path to the neighbouring

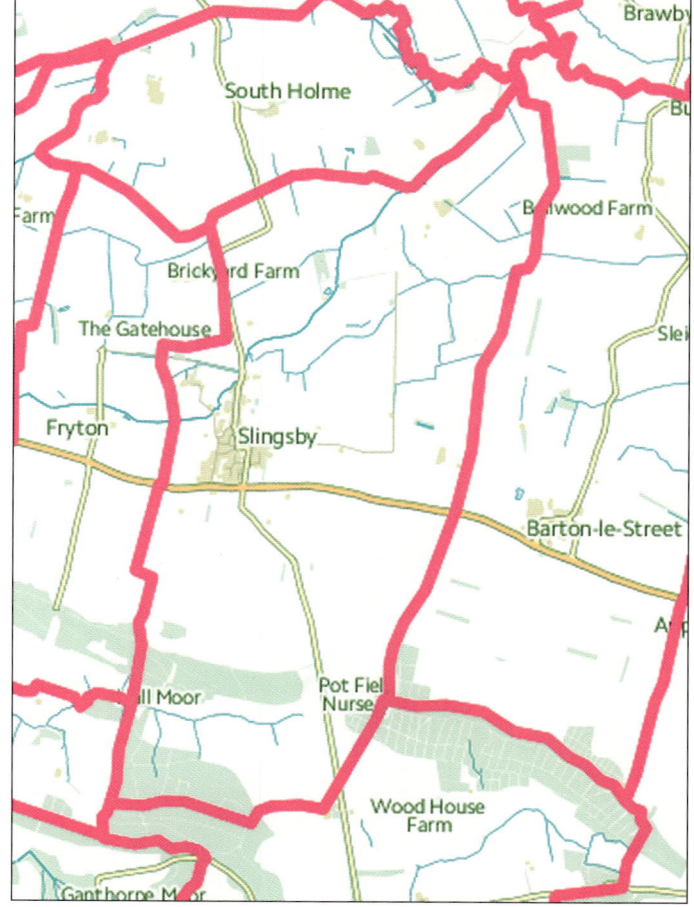

These are the boundaries of the parish of Slingsby in North Yorkshire as shown on the Ordnance Survey Election maps site.

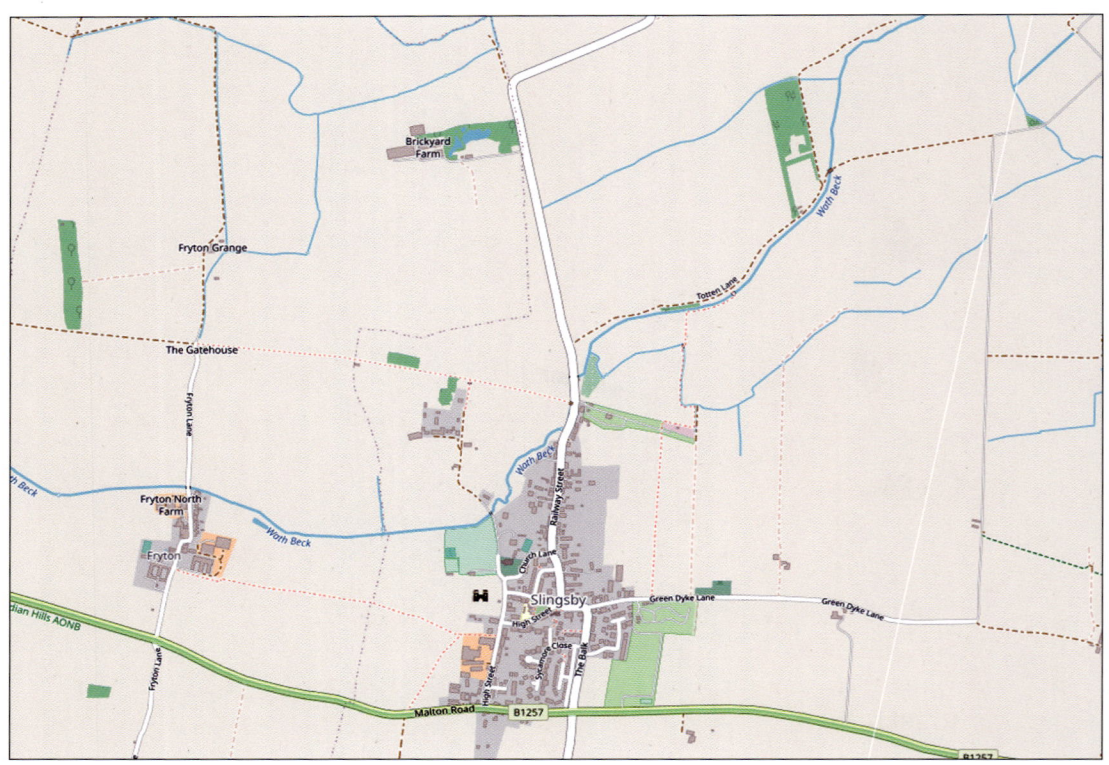

The same area as seen on a map. Note that with the exception of the two roads that cross the parish the other lanes all end at various farms and smallholdings. Also note, the pathways that extend from them to some of the other farms, these will be rights-of-way from ancient times.
(OpenStreetMap)

settlement might also be the one to the market, thereby becoming more used than some of the others, especially if further outlying settlements used it as a through route as well. So how were these paths delineated? The shortest route between two places is a straight line and I cannot conceive of people doing anything other than that, all other things being equal. However, detours may have been required for any number of reasons, for instance the need to ford a river or beck or avoid steep gradients or simply to keep out of a muddy spot. There was not the strict fencing-off of land at this time that there is today and paths probably went by the way of least resistance.

We now have an emerging picture of small areas growing and linking up with some paths used more than others depending on the destination. So now we reach another stage. Moving from one market town to another. In the same way that you could reach one market by going one way, to reach another you had a few choices. If you were on the main through path, you went the other way along it, alternatively you went to your local market then chose the road that went to the one you wanted or you could simply cut a corner by going through some of the neighbouring settlements in that general direction. The picture is now of market towns linked by paths, and smaller settlements also

These are the remains of an iron age settlement at Chysauster in Cornwall. Note how most of the pathways lead to one or other of the buildings rather than actually going anywhere else. (GEP)

linked by paths some of which may be more used than others if they happen to be on a route to one or other of the market towns. A very early development of A and B roads if you like.

What happened when somebody wanted to go somewhere? They would say, to get from A to B, I need to go to A and then pass through C, D and E. So, the route from A to B was the route from A to C, then C to D, Then D to E and E to B. Navigation must have gone along these lines for a very long time. Only two eras have purpose-built long-distance roads being built, the Roman and the Modern eras. The changes in the 17th and 18th centuries were more upgrading of existing routes.

If I am making it seem that this network sprang into place in the Iron Age, it almost certainly evolved and grew with the increasing population of Britain over a long period of time as the Neolithic hunter/gatherers gave way to Bronze Age farmers and continued to do so after the Iron Age.

What about long distance routes? Who needed them? There is very little existing evidence about the tribes of Britain prior to the Roman era but it seems that they were grouped into tribal kingdoms some of which may have had connections to other tribes in northern Europe. Let us take an example: the Brigantii. They occupied territory in modern day Yorkshire, Lancashire, Durham and Northumberland. At the time of the Roman invasion, Ptolemy names seven towns as belonging to the Brigantii. With the exceptions of York and Ilkley, these have remained small places or areas. (There were also Brigantii in Ireland, however, it is not known whether there was any connection.) This distribution however indicates that there must have been significant travel between these places. There must have

The Pre-Roman Era • 13

been messengers, traders, drovers, entertainers and maybe armies or religious processions.

Not many of the Iron Age roads remain as first the Romans and later generations either upgraded them or ploughed them over. There are however some remains that are known about and today these are generally given the name trackways or greenlanes. However, a word of caution – it is generally not possible to accurately date a green lane. There is no guarantee that your local green lane has been around since prehistoric times. Some of these routes had many pathways like the distributions of streams and rivers in a river delta, and they were not fenced in to a specific pathway until much later. One way of attempting

to date trackways is to note where all the prehistoric sites in an area are located and look at which roads or paths connect them up. This may be more difficult than first thought. I tried to do this between two hill forts in North Yorkshire, the earthworks at Aldro above Birdsall near Malton and Sutton Bank, a distance of approximately 30 miles. Now the main roads from Malton to Thirsk provide about 24 of those miles (via the B1257 and A170) and run pretty much direct. Certainly, part of this is a Roman road as indicated by Margary and, also, the presence of places called Appleton-le-Street and Barton-le-Street.

The word 'Street' is often an indicator of a Roman road. Did the Romans build on an earlier well-established track? The problems

The iron age hill fort at Aldro near Malton in North Yorkshire. (GEP)

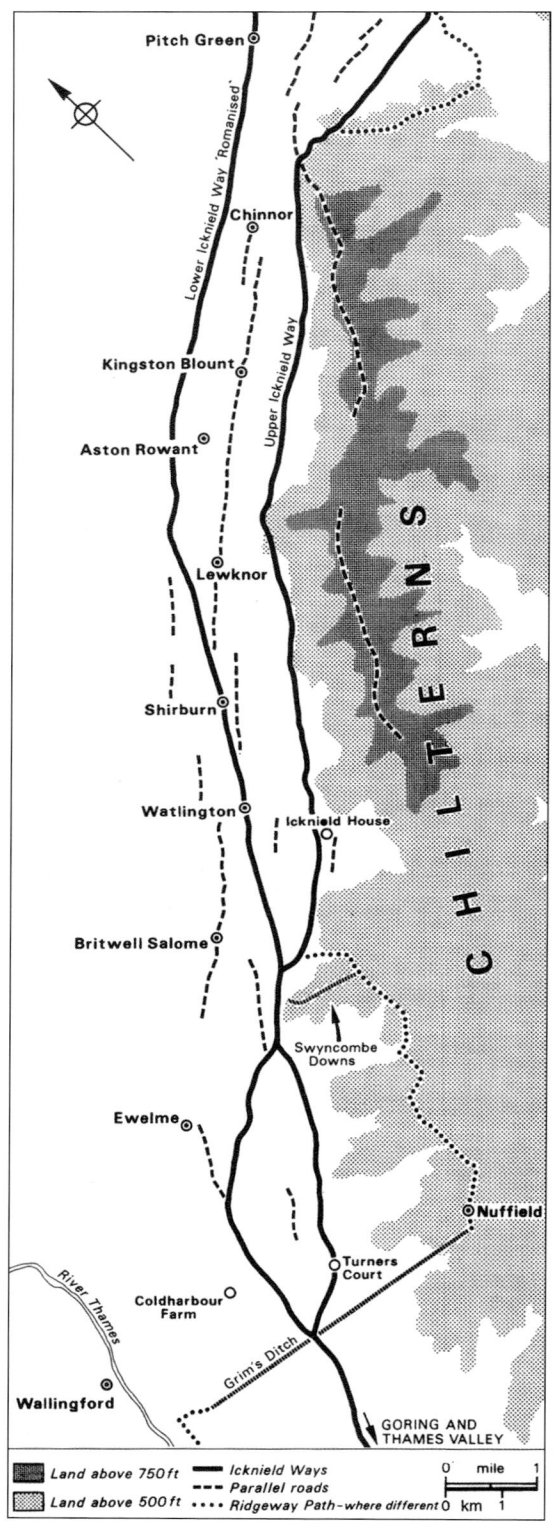

come when you try and join up this part to Aldro. In fact, a direct line from Aldro to Sutton Bank would not pass through Malton but three or four miles south. However, there are many steep slopes and a river in the way so it would not be surprising if the route went to Malton and on to an existing river crossing. Certainly, there was a Roman presence in what is now Malton in the first century so it would not be a great stretch to imagine a previous settlement. But the area is a mess of modern roads and pathways and bridleways none of which offer themselves up as obvious contenders. Therefore, I cannot come up with any definite route between the two.

One of the better known of these green ways is the Icknield Way which runs from Wiltshire to Suffolk although different sources disagree as to the exact route and there would again appear to have been alternative parallel routes in places. I do not see any problem with that, knowing the states of some roads in the 16th century I can well believe that different routes would have been used at different times depending on seasons or the presence of cattle drovers, etc. Some of this route has modern roads on it while other parts have disappeared. Much of the evidence is archaeological. It has been described as a 'belt studded with archaeological sites at irregular intervals'. Again, the route is semi-guessed at by the sites of the hill forts in the area.

This sketch by Paul Hindle from his *Road and Tracks for Historians* shows all the known sections of the Icknield Way along the Berkshire Chilterns, clearly showing a number of parallel routes.

A particular stretch of Icknield Way is known as The Ridgeway and can be seen across the Berkshire Downs between Overton Hill and the river Thames. People tended to use high ground as it afforded usually dry travel and the views allowed a measure of warning against possible trouble. There are hill forts along its route as in other places on the old roads. The modern Ridgeway Long Distance Footpath was

This is an engraving from William Stukeley in 1722 showing a view of the Foss Way looking south west from Crocolana, which was the Roman name for the hamlet of Brough (now bypassed) north east of Newark with its church steeple visible in the distance.
(Modern image GEP)

The Pre-Roman Era • 17

This is the village of Lacock in Wiltshire showing a typically rutted and muddy village street.

The same view today. Much improved. (GEP)

constructed in the early 1970s by linking up known parts of the old route in some cases selecting just one of the possible paths. It is only a general pointer to the original route.

It is quite frustrating looking for really very old roads as there is no definite evidence in most cases but the next stage in the development of Britain's roads is significantly easier to map.

ROMAN AND MEDIEVAL ROADS

THE ROMANS FIRST APPEARED in Britain in the first century BC as part of wars against Celtic tribes (another indication that there were links between British and European tribes). They did not reappear until 43AD and it took around 100 years for the country to be conquered south of mid-Scotland (the Antonine Wall).

So, what did the Romans do for us? Or at least for our roads? Well, the Romans were already accomplished engineers as their record still stands across Europe and the Middle East. They built large buildings, bridges, aqueducts, viaducts, and roads. Quite a lot of roads! We know there are thousands of miles of Roman highways identified across Europe, but what about Britain?

By all accounts there was an extensive road system in Britain. There were known long distance roads for instance Foss Way, Dere Street, Ermine Street, and others but it is believed that these names were given to those roads by the Anglo-Saxons that came later. It is not known what the Romans called those roads and unfortunately there are no maps. We can however trace them on the ground. The Romans built roads to a standard. This included building them on an 'agger' – that is a raised mound of earth of varying widths – some quite wide and as high as three or four feet from the surrounding area. There was usually a ditch at each side. The centre of this agger

This stone carving shows a Roman messenger on a road.

Another carving showing a Roman *carpentum*. A four wheeled carriage drawn by four horses. Roman streets were good enough to allow wheeled traffic in some comfort.

was made into a hard surface with two layers of stone, a layer of large stones covered by a layer of smaller stones to fill in the gaps. In some cases, they were even paved with stone. It seems that the roads were originally built for the military but not necessarily to and from the places where the fighting was taking place. The Foss Way for instance runs south-west to north-east between Lincoln and Axminster. This is likely to have been the front line at a point in the Roman advance across the country so the road permitted fast movement *along* the front line rather than to or from it.

Once again, it is very difficult to say whether a road today was Roman, the smaller local roads were probably like those that went before and came after without aggers and surfacing. The larger roads were often pillaged for their stone or else were ignored and not used. Others have been upgraded.

However, they exhibited one characteristic that does assist the modern-day researcher: the Romans built them straight . . . and I mean ruler straight! Roman long-distance roads tend to be long straights with occasional changes of alignment (bends to you and me!). The straightness of a modern road is of course not a definite

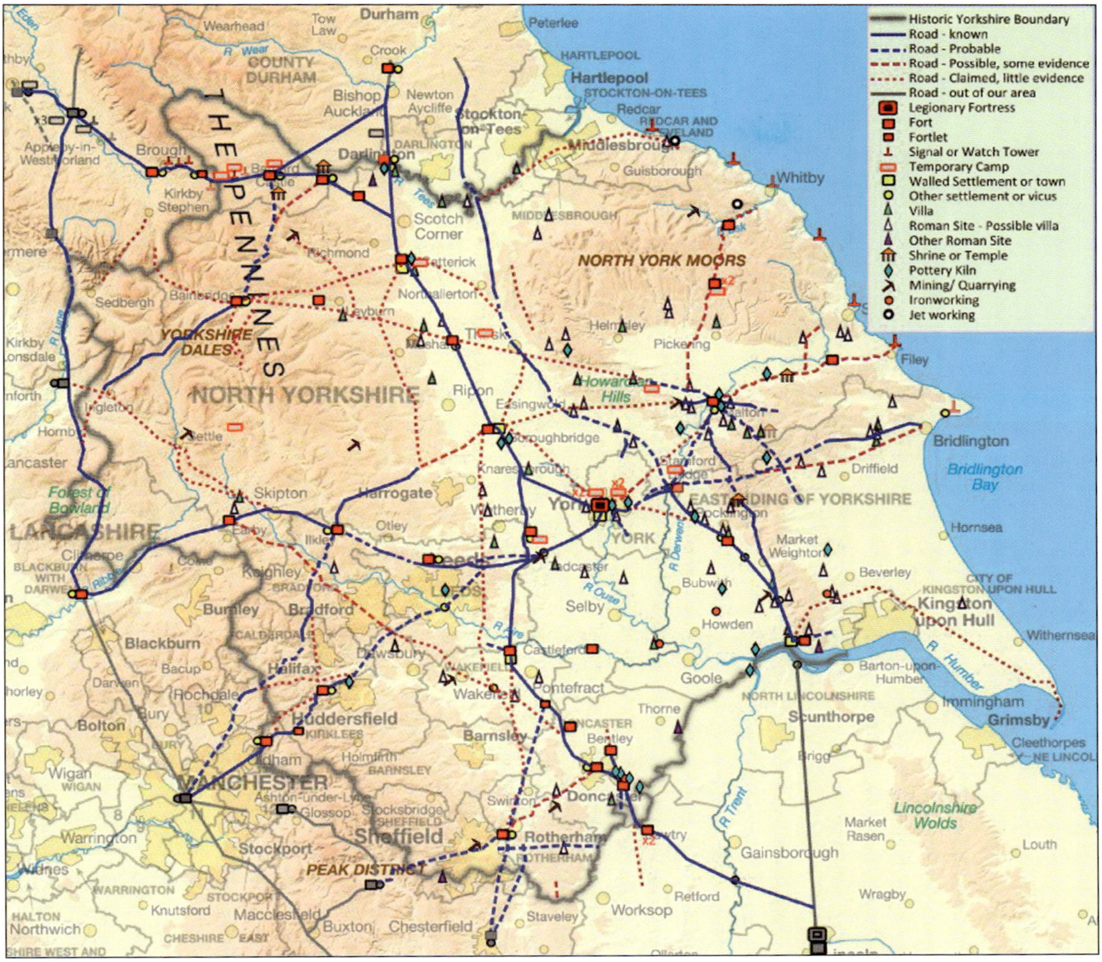

A map of Roman roads in Yorkshire. From the Roman Roads Research Association. (www.romanroads.org)

A typical Roman road showing its curved surface and the remains of its stone.

Roman and Medieval Roads • 21

Turf mark showing the course of Roman Ryknild street across fields.

sign of Roman activity as there are more recent reasons for straight roads but it may indicate something to be investigated.

Ivan Margary was a Sussex antiquarian and member of the Sussex Archaeological Society. He was clearly a Roman road enthusiast as he first published *Roman Roads in the Weald* and then his later work *Roman Roads in Britain* in the 1950s. The advent of aerial photography had made it easy to spot straight stretches of road that could then be investigated on the ground. Margary also created a cataloguing method for Roman roads a bit like the modern road numbering method. This is still in use today. *Roman Roads in Britain* is still the most complete work but there are modern local studies to add to it as of course technology has improved. Margary would have loved the internet and Google Streetview!

For example, say we find a straight road on the map that has not already been designated as Roman. Of course, most of the easy ones have already been investigated. The thing to do then is to go and have a look at one. I have tried this with a road near where I live. Currently the B1257, it is also known as Margary 814 (or M814). This stretch of road runs between Malton and Hovingham in North Yorkshire. The B1257 beyond Hovingham is not considered Roman but what I could not work out was, if it was Roman to Hovingham, why no further?

I first looked at the evidence for it being Roman because I know this piece of road very well and I know it has virtually no straight stretches at all! Malton was a well-known Roman fort with other roads in evidence and a road west from Malton would not be beyond belief. Also, on the B1257 there are villages called Appleton-le-Street and Barton-le-Street. The old Saxon word 'Streate' was apparently given to roads which were Roman in origin so such place names signify a Roman connection. Therefore, if it is Roman why is it not straight? I do not know the answer to this except possibly that the terrain is hilly and the road runs along a terrace on the edge of the Howardian Hills. Would they not have made the terrace a bit straighter? Interestingly, the current road runs along the edges of the villages along it rather than through them. There are footpaths between the villages lower down the hill that are straighter than the B1257. Were these once a Roman way? I am speculating of course, there would need to be archaeological evidence.

I then addressed the fact that it stops at Hovingham. Well perhaps it did not. Some of the things to look for in investigating a possible Roman road are nearby known Roman sites to which they may have given access and for further stretches of straight road. Arriving in Hovingham the road takes a sharp turn to the right and heads north towards Helmsley. Just after this right turn however is an unclassified road off to the left that would theoretically be the continuation of M814. So, is there any evidence? Well, yes. There is the site of a Roman villa on the right almost immediately, and several possible Roman tumuli in the area. Also, about a mile up this road is a place called Coldharbour. This name (also related to Caldicot) is not uncommon in Britain and is thought to be a Saxon term referring to ruined earlier possibly military buildings where some shelter on the road could be obtained. Further on in the Yearsley area there are some long straights. All in all, there are some indicators that the way could have continued in this general direction but where to? Thirsk is the obvious answer but Thirsk is believed to have been founded by the Saxons after the Roman occupation.

So, you can see the difficulties involved. Without being able to excavate it, one cannot positively identify a stretch of road so you cannot say for certain. As I have mentioned before, I am not a historian or archaeologist so that is beyond my remit. I would still like to know though.

What we can do however is to follow a well-known Roman road. The Foss Way stretches from Lincoln to Axminster and nowhere on that 200-mile run does it deviate more than six miles from a straight line drawn between the two.

We will start at the northern end in Lincoln where the Foss Way starts at the south gate of the Roman town on the High Street, approximately where the later Stonebow gate stands and heads due south as the B1262, the High Street becoming St Catherines. At the bottom of St Catherines is a fork. The Foss Way goes off to the right

Stonebow gate at the southern end of the High Street in Lincoln and the northern end of the Foss Way. Stonebow comes from an Old Norse word 'stennibogi' meaning 'stone arch'. Interestingly there is also a Stonebow in York, that most Viking of cities although the street is quite a recent addition so I do not know if that name is also connected to the Old Norse. (GEP)

as the A1434 Newark Road and the left fork goes south eventually to London as Ermine Street. It could be said then that the stretch between this point and Lincoln is a multiplex of the Foss Way and Ermine Street.

After the fork, Foss Way heads down to Bracebridge where it turns sharp right to cross the River Witham. Once the road straightens out it heads in an almost dead straight line for Newark becoming the A46 where the modern ring road meets it. The only place where the modern road diverts off it is where it bypasses Brough village. We then cross the A1 and go straight through Newark as the B6166 crossing the Great North Road by Newark Castle. At the other side we rejoin the A46 and head south-west through Farndon and East Stoke. The Foss Way runs alongside us in places as the A46 was dualled in 2012 and some stretches were left as local access roads. Apart from those, the A46 does not deviate from the Foss Way except where there is a small parting of the ways near Willoughby.

On the outskirts of Leicester, the A46 leaves us and we go on straight into Leicester still on a straight line, skirting Syston and becoming the A607 Melton Road. We go into Leicester city centre on Belgrave Gate and the Haymarket. Where the Haymarket joins Church Gate, the road curves right into the now pedestrianised High Street. This is where the Roman gate in the city wall used to stand. We run straight down the High Street to exit at the west gate crossing the river Soar and going down Duns Lane and Braunstone Gate to become the A5460. Foss Way follows this to the Leicester ring-road and from here things get a little more confusing as our road is reduced to stubs and small stretches of minor roads and even footpaths in places.

We go through Narborough on the B4114 but at Stoney Bridge the Foss Way takes a left fork and becomes a minor road that peters out in some fields becoming a field boundary and a farm track. We can pick it up again at High Cross on the A5 that was the crossing point of Foss Way and Watling Street. Taking the B4455 from this crossroads puts us back on track. We can follow the B4455 for a long distance past Coventry and Leamington Spa. Having driven along this road I can attest that its narrow and sunken in places, and at almost every crossroads it is not the priority road so you have to stop each time.

Eventually we come out onto the A429 that becomes Foss Way and we follow it all the way to Cirencester, another Roman town. It leaves Cirencester on the A429 but that disappears off to the left to leave us on the A433 and not far after this once again Foss Way leaves modern roads at the airfield at Kemble. It goes under the airport and is then traceable as farm tracks and field boundaries. It resumes as a minor road some 12 miles further south, just north of the M4 near Sherston. These minor roads eventually approach Bath on high ground and descend to the river at Batheaston.

Its route into Bath is on the A4 and A3039. We cross the River Avon on the old bridge and leave town up Holloway joining the A367 and heading south-west. The road is less straight in this area as it deals with geographical obstacles. We go through Peasedown and Radstock

Below, right and overleaf: A number of views of the Foss Way threading its dead straight route through Britain. At various times dual carriageway, S2 and pathways. (GEP)

Foss Way leaving Lincoln looking south west. (GEP)

Foss Way as a dual carriageway in Lincolnshire. (GEP)

An overhead view of High Cross. Foss Way's crossing with Watling Street on the Leicestershire/Warwickshire border. The north east arm of Fossway has disappeared here but we can follow it on pathways nearby. (GEP)

Another view of Foss Way in Wiltshire looking south east. Now it's pathways and bridleways unlike the dual carriageway in Lincolnshire. It does in fact form part of the Gloucestershire/Wiltshire border in this area indicating its former importance. (GEP)

and Foss Way cuts a straight line off the A367 to Shepton Mallet and then heads south as the A37 as far as Ilchester. There it joins the A303 for a short distance but at South Petherton it branches off again into minor roads and paths. It is more difficult to follow as the terrain is very hilly but it runs from Dinnington to Chillington where it briefly joins the A30 before heading south on the B3167 which joins the A358 to Axminster.

Many folks have the Foss Way linking Lincoln and Exeter. While there is a Roman road traceable between Axminster via Kilmington and Honiton to Exeter I am not convinced that it constitutes part of the Foss Way; rather the continuation of an east-west road coming from Dorchester. On the coast near Axminster is a small place called Seaton. This was a Roman port so I suspect Foss Way continued up to there. This would make Axminster the crossing point of the two roads, a place where towns often grew.

So, we can see that by following the course of a former Roman main road 2,000 years later, parts of it make up every type of modern road . . . from footpath up to dual carriageway. This highlights the difficulty of looking at a road and trying to work out when it was built as the dual carriageways could be on the line of a road as old as the Foss Way or could be completely new roads. Likewise, a farm track might have been a major road at one time. Remembering that even a major road in the past would still seem like a modern minor road to us.

After around 400 years, the Roman occupation ended and the era of the Saxon and Norseman took over. Historians and archaeologists generally agree that Roman rule in Britain ended around 410AD. There is evidence that things had been deteriorating in previous years that probably had a lot to do with increasing raids by Saxons from the Germanic part of Europe. By the year 600AD lowland Britain was a much different place. The Romano-British had been effectively driven into the west and the Anglo-Saxon had taken over. Not without his own problems, the Scandinavian Norsemen were also invading and they fought back and forward for the next three centuries. The Norsemen almost won but were pushed back until eventually they held the north (the Danelaw) and the Saxons held the south. Eventually, in 1066, a pair of decisive battles sorted it out once and for all and stability broke out. Well for a while anyway.

The invaders were in the main sea-going folk and had little use for roads. They also had little use for urban areas. The upshot of this was that many Roman towns became deserted and fell into ruin as did some of the roads that led to them. They did however have one use that has lasted to the present day: the aggers of the Roman roads were very visible. The Romans would have kept the roads clear of vegetation and so they would have been a major part of the landscape. Thus, they were very handy for providing boundaries between estates and many a modern parish today has a boundary that butts up onto what was a Roman road. Interestingly our parish map in Chapter 2 is an exception to this. The B1257 mentioned earlier runs through it as well as several other parishes rather than along their boundaries.

So how did our invaders get around? Well pretty much as the pre-Roman folk, by horse and on foot. Baggage and cargo appear to have been put on pack-horses rather than carts so we have the problem from our point of view that we can no longer designate any road as particularly dating from that period. It seems clear that many of the major Roman ways were used although for some reason newer settlements tended to avoid them. Eventually they succumbed to hundreds of years of use and neglect, becoming rutted tracks or even holloways which occurred where an entire road surface sank under the weight of traffic. There are Holloway Road names all over England, most notably as part of the Great North Road in north London. Some of course were upgraded in later periods, these upgrades destroying anything left of the Roman engineering.

We are once again left with the ongoing problem that we simply cannot say when a road came into being. I must also stress that nothing from this period or before remotely resembles a modern major road. They would all seem like small lanes to us.

The medieval period can be said to have started in 1066 and extended to the Tudor period around 1500. During this period society moved slowly and painfully towards something resembling what we know today. There were periods of stability and periods of instability such as the Stephen-Matilda civil war (1135-1154), the Baron's War (1215-17) or the Black Death in 1348-1350.

Who travelled during this period? Well armies for a start. Also, religious travellers and pilgrims. Merchants and supply trains. Messengers, taxmen, sheriffs and other officials. And the Court. Kings in this period tended to move around from place to place as the court was a large organisation that quickly exhausted the resources of a local area. During my research I came across a website (http://neolography.com/timelines/JohnItinerary.html) which had an interactive timeline and a map upon which were plotted the stopping places of King John and his court for every day of his reign. Very interesting, it gives an idea of the route taken between each place. Paul Hindle in his *Medieval Roads and Tracks* also addresses

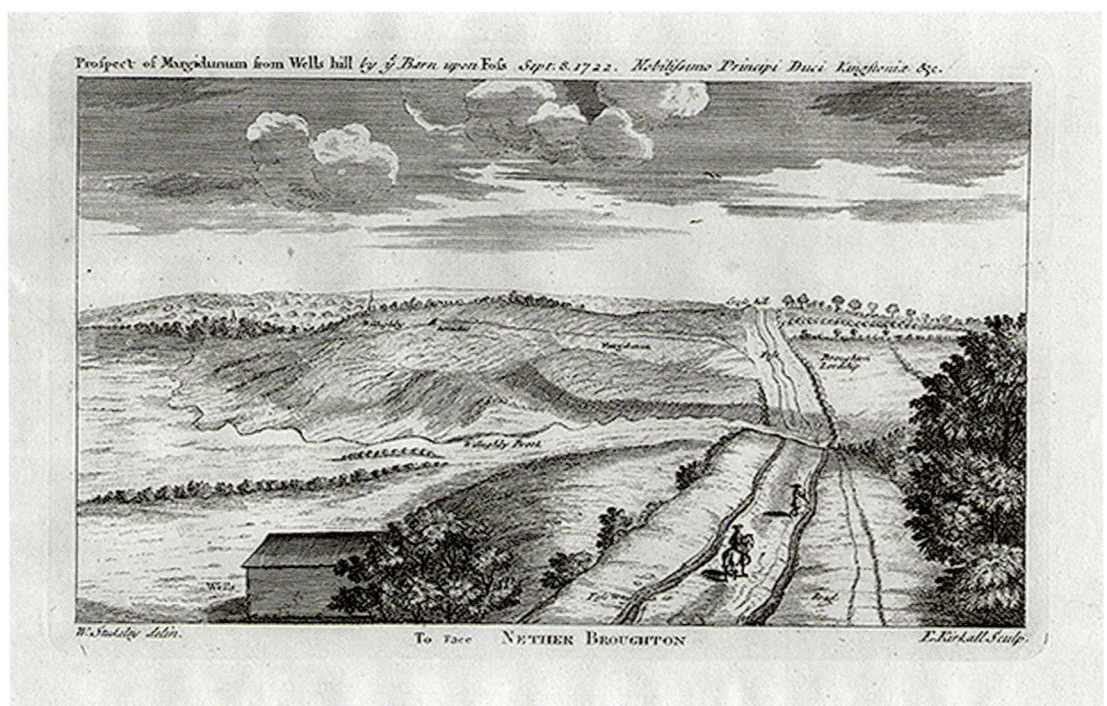

A sketch by William Stukeley which shows the Foss Way south west of Newark near the Roman town of Margidunum as was. Not far from here the final battle of the Wars of the Roses was fought at East Stoke. Perhaps indicating Foss Way's importance as a north-south route.

This comparison is around the right place looking south on the old A46 which runs alongside the A46 dual carriageway. The junction is named after the old Roman town.

this issue. He states that 'it is reasonable to suppose that if a king used certain routes frequently then some reasonable road or track must have existed'.

So let us have a look. John, in March 1200, moved from Woodstock near Oxford via Silverstone to Northampton and then north to

Roman and Medieval Roads • 31

Clipstone and Tickhill near Doncaster. Starting at Woodstock it does not take much imagination to follow a route on the modern A4095, B430 and A43 to Northampton. However, digging a little deeper shows us a stretch of the old Roman Akeman Street running just north of Woodstock. This goes to Banbury where another Roman way runs north to Silverstone. Remembering that this was probably the larger road at the time, did John use the old Roman route? We cannot of course prove which way John went and this once again shows the difficulty of knowing where the roads used actually were.

Unfortunately, as evidence goes, it is fairly thin and there is very little documentary evidence of the existence of any particular road. People wrote about the travellers, the method of travel itself or the state of the roads, there were no descriptions of the roads or routes themselves. Presumably the traveller of yore took as little notice in those days of what was under their feet . . . just as today's travellers are little concerned as to what is under their wheels. What evidence exists is usually of a secondary nature, e.g. a mention of a particular road in a documented court case or charter. This does prove that a particular road was in use at that time if nothing else but it does not tell us how long that road has been in use.

Some roads were named to indicate what particular type of traffic used it. For instance, *portways* were often routes taken to markets or ports, the carriage of merchandise. Bearing in mind that many of the medieval officials wrote in French, I suspect the word comes from the French verb *porter* which means to carry. There were also *herepaths* or army roads indicating the movements of Saxon armies, *here* being a Saxon/Old English word for army (the modern German word for army is *Heer*); church or monastic ways, saltways and droveways which were where animals were driven to markets. In the days without refrigeration, cattle had to be moved to the market before slaughter which meant they had to walk there. There was a general movement towards towns and from the north and west of the country to the south and east. Droving carried on until the mid-1800s. Place names and other names are also an indication of the use of a route, for example Water Stratford indicates the Ford on the Street (Roman Road) giving an indication that the road was a Roman one. The Drovers pub or the Heifer pubs were probably on a drove road.

I do suspect however that these roads were not specifically used by the named industries. If a path existed and was the most convenient way from A to B, then I would think that most travellers would use it.

A village in North Yorkshire showing a pretty standard rural road of the early 20th Century. They were all like this at one time. Including the obligatory dollop of horse manure.

Roman and Medieval Roads • 33

It was probably given a name for convenience, the possible exception being drove ways as I can see good reasons why travellers would want to stay away from huge herds of cattle on their journey!

By the early 1500s, Britain was well on the way to being recognisable to a modern reader. Most of the towns and villages were established and if a map of the road system existed, we would probably be able to trace most of the roads on a modern map. They would of course only be the minor roads or even footpaths on our modern map except where they have been upgraded. We have a situation where the parish system described in Chapter 2 has spread to cover the entire country. So far, the system has withstood the pressure of population growth. There are no records of major problems at this time and it is clear from the itineraries that travel took place at all times of the year and as we saw King John moved around extensively and at some speed. This would indicate that travel was not difficult and undertaken as a matter of course.

CHANGES 1500 – 1700

A SNAPSHOT OF A road in the mid-16th century would show what we would call tracks. They would not be fenced or hedged in to allow travellers to pick their own path around any swampy spots or up a gradient. There would be no surface dressing or drainage. A road was not so much a physical thing as a right of passage, meaning that the traveller had the right to pass that way, and there was not necessarily a laid down track. Obviously as routes were used more frequently then, a clear path would emerge. We can make several observations about roads at this time, and Paul Hindle does just this in his *Roads and Tracks for Historians*.

> 'First, many Roman Roads remained in use, still providing the easiest way across the country. Second, new medieval roads came into being simply through habitual use. Third, the road system as a whole was adequate for the amount of traffic that existed, even in winter. Fourth, roads often acted as feeders for the river system for the movement of heavy or bulky merchandise. Finally, it is clear that many of today's major roads were created or used in the medieval period, simply because of the need to service great growth of agriculture, industry and trade.'

However, things were about to change. In 1485, the house of Tudor took over the monarchy and a long period of economic growth began which set into motion the changes that were about to happen to the country's roads. Over the next 300 years a number of different major and ongoing factors changed the face of our roads forever. As it is difficult to deal with these changes in a chronological fashion because they were happening concurrently, we will take each from its approximate starting point.

The first event – which may appear inconsequential – was the dissolution of the monasteries by Henry VIII. The monks from these monasteries had provided a certain amount of repair work on roads, river crossings and bridges. This now ceased although the repercussions were not immediately apparent. Another consequence of the dissolution was that John Leland, an antiquarian with the ear of the King did a lot of travelling. He journeyed to most of the dissolved monasteries to catalogue their libraries and, being a writer, he also described his travels. His writings have survived and have been published as John Leland's *Itinerary* giving us a unique description of travel in the 16th century. He does not discuss the roads themselves, implying that they were 'normal', i.e. unremarkable at that time.

The economic climate in the 16th and 17th centuries was the kickstart to what followed. A number of factors, unique to Britain during this time, led to entrepreneurial growth, creating population growth and consumerism, finally culminating in the industrial revolution of the mid-1700s. Although this is an *extremely* simplified statement, one thing in particular had a direct bearing on the roads.

In the Tudor period, economic factors and farming practises led to something called 'enclosures'. This came about when farmland, which up until that point had been arable and common land, was fenced in. While it created much larger fields, at the same time it dispossessed peasant farmers and in some cases whole villages. Again, this is a very simplified version of events but enclosure spelled the end of the open field system prevalent until that time. As far as farming was concerned, it made economic sense for the landowners but it upset any number of villagers and commoners and there were riots.

An engraving of the Great North Road in Highgate, note how wide it is and clear tracks over the whole width.

So how does this affect our road system? As noted earlier, the existence of a road up until that time implied a right-of-way but now a physical road was actually designated. Often used as a boundary between farms or estates, the road was left as a fenced off area between fields, much as they are today but this was the first time that this had been the case. Some enclosure roads are easy to spot as originally they were left quite wide – usually around 60 feet – between the hedges or fences to facilitate easy movement of animals. The modern road does not need to be so wide so today you often see a tarmaced lane with very wide grass verges. They were also built as straight as possible but should not be mistaken for Roman alignments. Enclosures created great social upheaval. While it provided people for the industrial power-houses starting to spring up during this time, thus helping the coming industrial revolution and accelerating growth, it also created more traffic.

Another invention arrived from Europe in the late Tudor period: the coach! Up until this point, wheeled vehicles were rare, especially in the north of the country. They were unsuitable for long distance work as horses were not strong enough to pull laden wagons any distance over the rough roads of the time and oxen were too slow. As noted earlier, much of the transport of goods was undertaken by pack horse or by river or sea. The coach was a light, fast vehicle, initially suspended by leather straps, and could be pulled by four horses. They quickly

This is the B5305 in Cumbria. A clear example of an enclosure road. Note the wide hedges and big verges. (CC)

became popular and by the late 1600s there was the beginnings of a regular coach service from London to many outlying places.

Among other aspects that were developing at this time were science and technology. In the early 1500s, the science of surveying gained new instruments and procedures, including the theodolite and triangulation. Map-makers were starting to produce accurate maps. In the 1570s Christopher Saxton produced the first county maps but, while they had the towns and villages in the right places, they did not include the roads in between. We had to wait another 100 years for that. John Ogilby produced Britain's first road atlas in 1675 called *The Britannia Atlas*. It consisted of 100 plates of strip maps showing the routes from place to place with many of them starting from London and others starting from places marked on the London-based maps.

I decided to see if it was possible to trace these maps on a current atlas so first, I chose as my destination, King's Lynn. Ogilby Plate 43 is the one that ends at King's Lynn but it begins at Puckeridge which is a small village in Hertfordshire. So, if we then look at the plates from London to see which London route goes through Puckeridge, we find that it is Plate 5 to Stilton. A traveller who wanted to go from London to King's Lynn would use Plate 5 as far as Puckeridge and then Plate 43 to reach the destination.

The Ogilby plates show a road from bottom to top with side roads, rivers and places marked. Also, the topography is indicated with up slopes shown as an upright hill and down slopes as an upside-down hill. Miles are marked on the road at every mile, and every furlong (1/8 mile) by a dot.

So where does Plate 5 start? The left-hand strip has the road leaving a large urban area simply designated 'London'. This is not the London that we know of course because four miles further along is Newington, a place we would now consider to be well and truly within London. In 1675, however, it most certainly was not. Side roads are shown leading to Hackney and Islington with the distances to each. Hoxton and Kingsland are shown as blips on the road so it's clear we are on the modern A10. This is not surprising at it is the Old North Road that predated the Great North Road and is based on the Roman Ermine Street. We head north past Tottenham. Interestingly Ogilby has labelled this Tottenham Street, possibly a reference to the Roman way? Past Tottenham, the modern A10 leaves us branching off to the left, and the old A10 has now been renamed the A1010. We proceed through other places I would expect to see leaving London on the current A1010: Edmonton, Lower Edmonton, Ponders End, Enfield Highway and Enfield Wash; then all villages out in the country, even

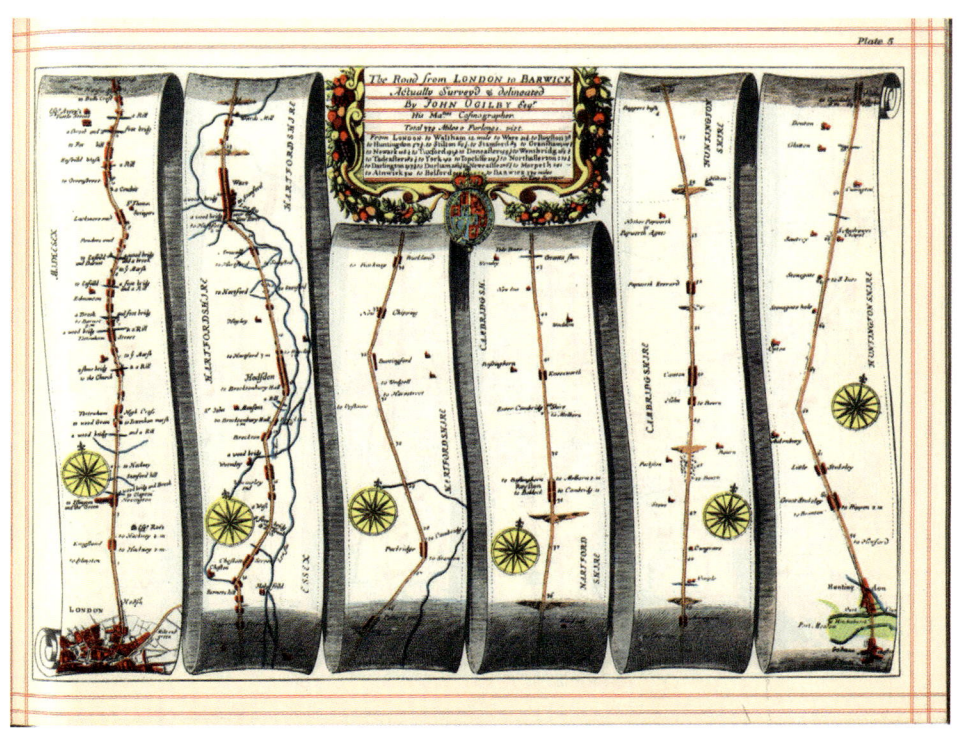

The two Ogilby strip maps used to go from London to Kings Lynn.

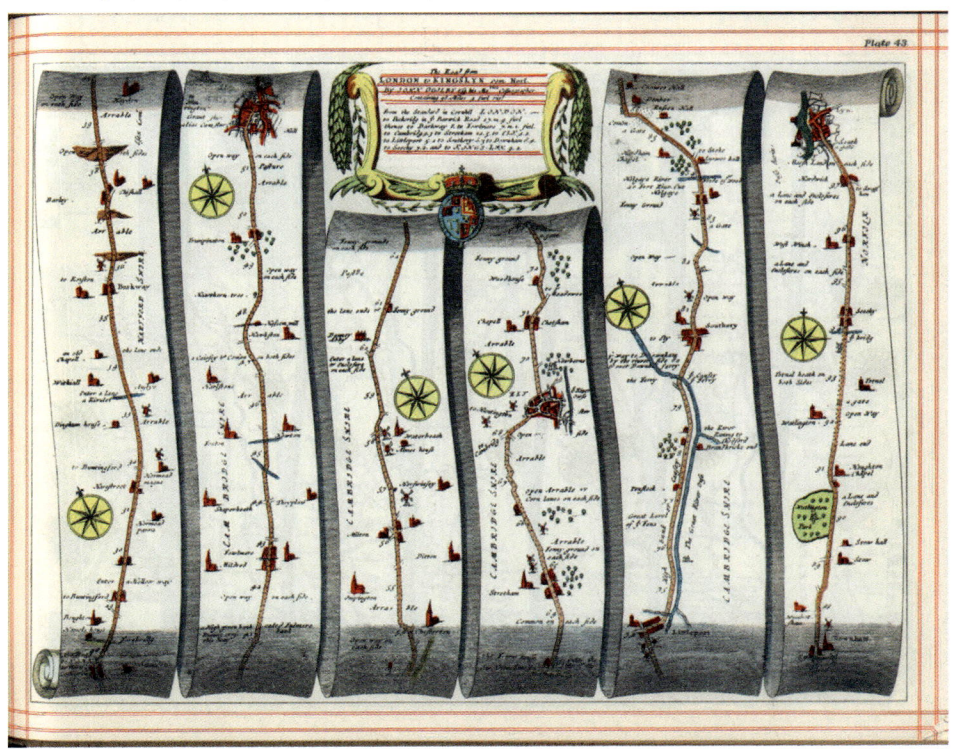

Changes 1500 – 1700 • 39

on a map dated 1876. This ends the first strip so we move across to the bottom of the next one and carry on our journey.

One problem with the strip maps is that they are stylised as scrolls. This means that the ends are rolled over and shaded slightly which makes it difficult to read the very start and end of each scroll. The first place identifiable on the second strip is Turners Hill which no longer exists as a place name, but part of the B176 just south of Cheshunt is called Turners Hill. This means that Waltham Cross must be lurking in the shaded area between strips. We follow it north from Cheshunt through Turnford, Wormley (the B176 has now become the A1170), Brockton (Broxbourne), Hodsden (Hoddesden), Hailey and Amwell into Ware. We leave Ware on the A1170 which quickly becomes an unclassified road through Wadesmill and Colliers End to Puckeridge. We are now 27½ miles from where we set off in London and it's time to take the Cambridge Road from Puckeridge on Plate 43.

Plate 43 starts at Puckeridge, hiding in the shadow at the bottom of the scroll. We are still at the 28-mile mark showing that the distances are still measured from London. The north road forks at the top end of the village and Ermine Street leaves us at the left fork. The first recognisable place name on the road north of Puckeridge is Hare Street which confirms we are on the modern B1368. There are a couple of unnamed villages before that which I presume to be Braughing and Hay Street. We pass through Barkway and Barley and Fowlmere with no mention that we have crossed the Icknield Way between Barley and Fowlmere. North of Fowlmere we rejoin the modern A10 at Harston for a mile or so and then head into Trumpington on the A1309. There are two more miles of open country at the top of the second scroll before we arrive in Cambridge, 51½ miles from London.

Chesterton and Milton are the next two place names confirming that we are back on the A10 north of Cambridge. We pass Waterbeach to Stretham. Stretham is another indicator of a Roman road and, sure enough, Ermine Street has rejoined us just north of Waterbeach. The map indicates 'Fenny ground' on both sides in several places. Interestingly it also notes where 'a lane' begins and where it ends, this being an indication of an enclosure. Where there is no lane indicated, it would have been the old-style unfenced road.

We arrive at Ely which is shown with a recognisable street map and leave on the unclassified road via Chettisham to Littleport. We stay on the unclassified road north of Littleport because although the modern A10 runs up the east bank of the Great Ouse River, our way is clearly shown on the west bank concurrent with the minor road that runs there. We eventually cross the Ouse by ferry at a place where there is a farm – not surprisingly called Ferry Farm – and join the A10 on the other side. We stay on the A10 except for passing through both Southery and Hilgay and the other side of the river we take the dog-leg through Fordham and into Denver and Downham Market. North out of Downham Market we cut through Stow Bardolph and rejoin the A10. Soon arriving at what is now the major road junction

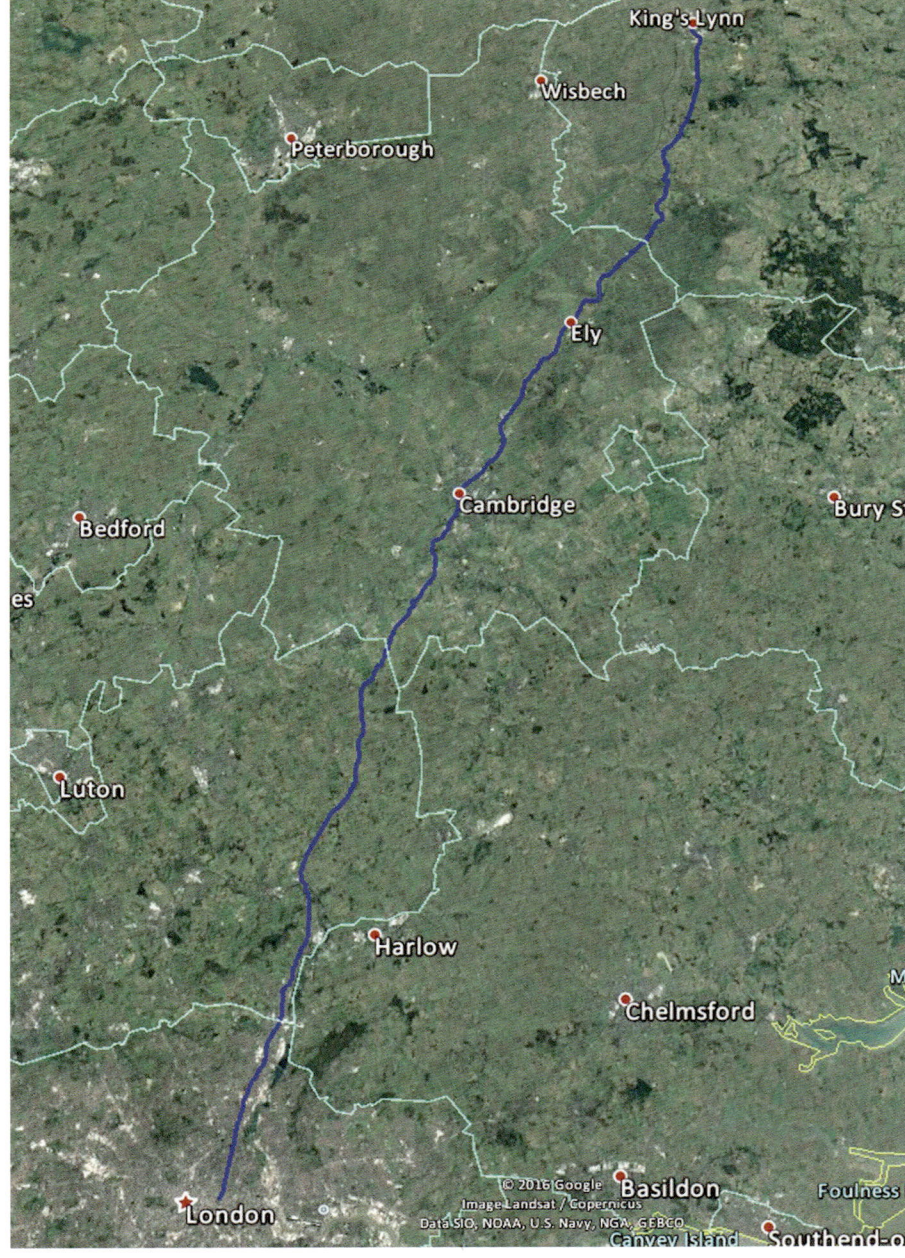

Ogilby's route from London to Kings Lynn superimposed on Google Earth Pro.

This lane north of Littleport was once the main road to Kings Lynn. (GEP)

of the A10, A47 and A149, we take the A149 into King's Lynn, arriving at the south gate on London Road.

Plotting this route on Google Earth throws up some interesting observations. Almost every inch of this route lies on a modern tarmaced road. None of it is a footpath or a farm track like parts of the Foss Way discussed earlier. The inference is that the road system was already established by 1675 . . . 350 years ago. The only changes are where villages and towns have been bypassed to through traffic by later upgrades. At one time, travellers needed regular stops for refreshment and horse changes but, as traffic increased and got faster, such regular stops were no longer needed and the through traffic was just causing delays in the villages. I also looked at this route on the earliest Ordnance Survey maps from the late 1800s. It is interesting to note that nearly all the modern changes have been carried out since then, in other words in the last 100 years. Also, most of the urban expansion has taken place since then too.

As a matter of interest, I was very surprised when I looked at one of the other sheets. As long as I can remember – and I have been driving on Britain's roads for over 40 years – the A38 has been the road from the Midlands to the West Country via Worcester, Gloucester and Bristol until surpassed by the M5. It also runs mostly on a Roman alignment and takes the easy route along the flat land alongside the Severn estuary north of Bristol. So, if asked what the original route from Gloucester to Bristol was, I would say that it was the route now followed by the A38 and leave it at that. However, when tracing it on Ogilby Plate 59, the A38 appears not to be the preferred route.

42 • HIGHWAYS OF BRITAIN – THEN AND NOW

Instead, we leave Gloucester's south gate and take Bristol Road which becomes the B4008 before it joins up with the modern A38 at Hardwicke. We stay on the A38 as far as Cambridge, but then we divert off it through Cambridge village onto the aptly-named Dursley road which then terminates in a dead end up against the M5. Before the M5 was built we would have carried on down this road, now the A4135 via Upper Cam into Dursley but then things get a bit confusing. Ogilby clearly has us turning off the A4135 just as we arrive at Dursley in an almost westerly direction. The landscape here is of a very hilly nature, which is shown on Ogilby's map, but there are no definite place names through which the road passes except a mention of a Nibley Park. The next on our route is Tortworth which is about four miles south-west of Dursley, although I am sure I can identify the river crossing at Damery. So where do we go between Dursley and Damery crossing? As Ogilby gives us enough information on the places to the left and right of our route, I can say that we probably pass to the north of North Nibley. He also indicates we climb and descend a steep hill which would be consistent with crossing Nibley Knoll. The only other clue is a place name which appears to be 'Titworth' which should be somewhere in the area between Damery and Nibley although I cannot find anything, not even a farm with that name.

After a lot of investigation, I have come up with two possibilities, both of which have us leaving Dursley on Hill Road which becomes The Broadway – an old name for a main road. At the top of the Broadway there is a path leading to Stancombe Farm that is in about the right place. We then follow some minor roads and arrive in Nibley Green but from here it is more unclear. Starting at the other end, north of Damery Crossing, Ogilby has us going through some woodland and then the road takes a sharp 90-degree right turn. This would be consistent with us following the unnamed road from Damery, through Michael Wood and following it round to the right by Middle and Upper Wick farms, which then leads to Nibley Green. However, this does strike me as a slightly long way round so an alternative solution would be to follow the lane from Nibley Green round the foot of the hill as far as Bassett Court where a footpath leads fairly directly past Katherine's Farm and Michaelwood Lodge Farm to Damery crossing but it does not have the wood or the right-hand bend. South of Tortworth our route becomes the B4058 and enters Bristol without returning to the A38.

This example is unlike our earlier one. Although this one can be mostly plotted on modern roads, there is this section that

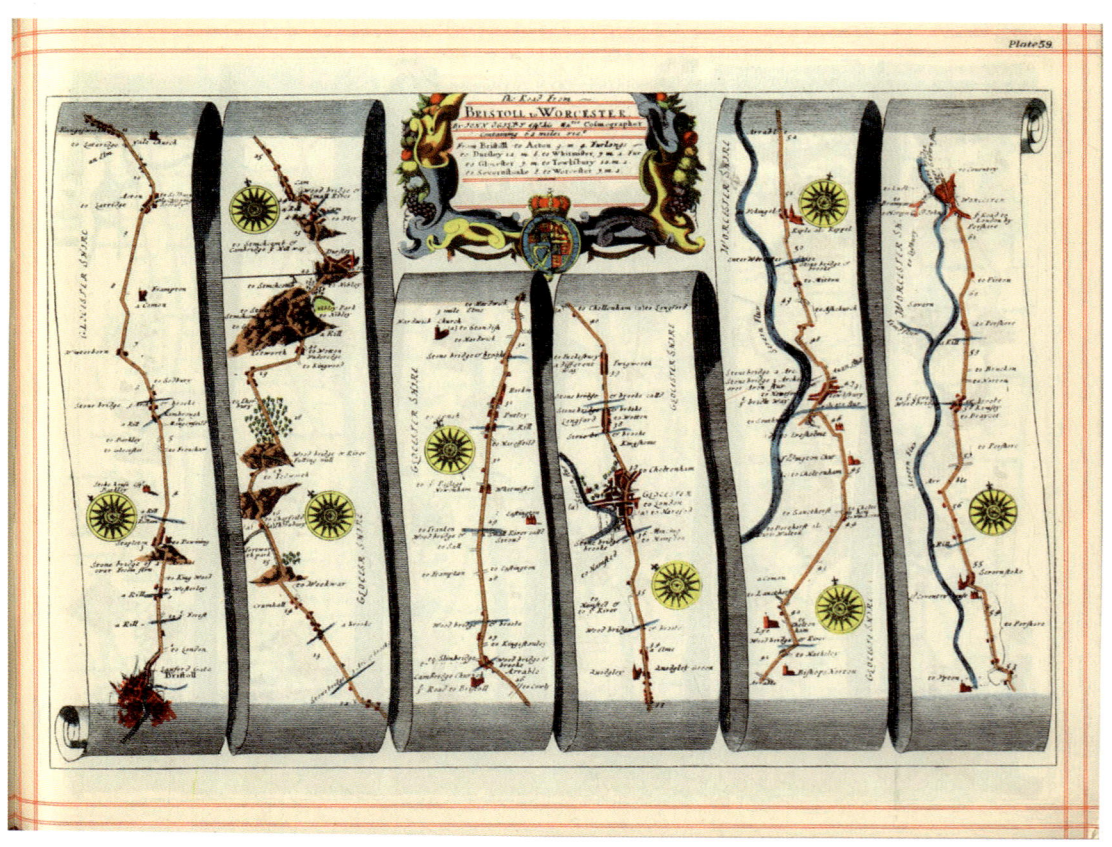

The strip map showing the route from Bristol to Worcester.

is unclear. And why did it divert from the A38 route? Ogilby notes at Cambridge village that a road off to the right is the 'road to Bristoll'. This would be the continuation of the A38 route so they were certainly aware of it. Why then travel by a route which was topographically more difficult? To that I do not know the answer. John Leland, writing over 100 years before Ogilby, also notes travelling between Dursley and Tortworth although unfortunately he does not elaborate on the exact route. [Some 2 or 3 years after this chapter was first written, I did solve the Dursley conundrum. It was to do with Ogilby putting Tortworth in the wrong place. The place he calls Tortworth is in fact Nibley Green!]

We are clear that by the 16th century there was a comprehensive road network in Britain, and that it was capable of handling the traffic that used it. However, it is also clear that with the increases in road use the roads quite quickly deteriorated. By the time of Ogilby in 1675, accounts of the dreadful state of roads were common. It was regarded

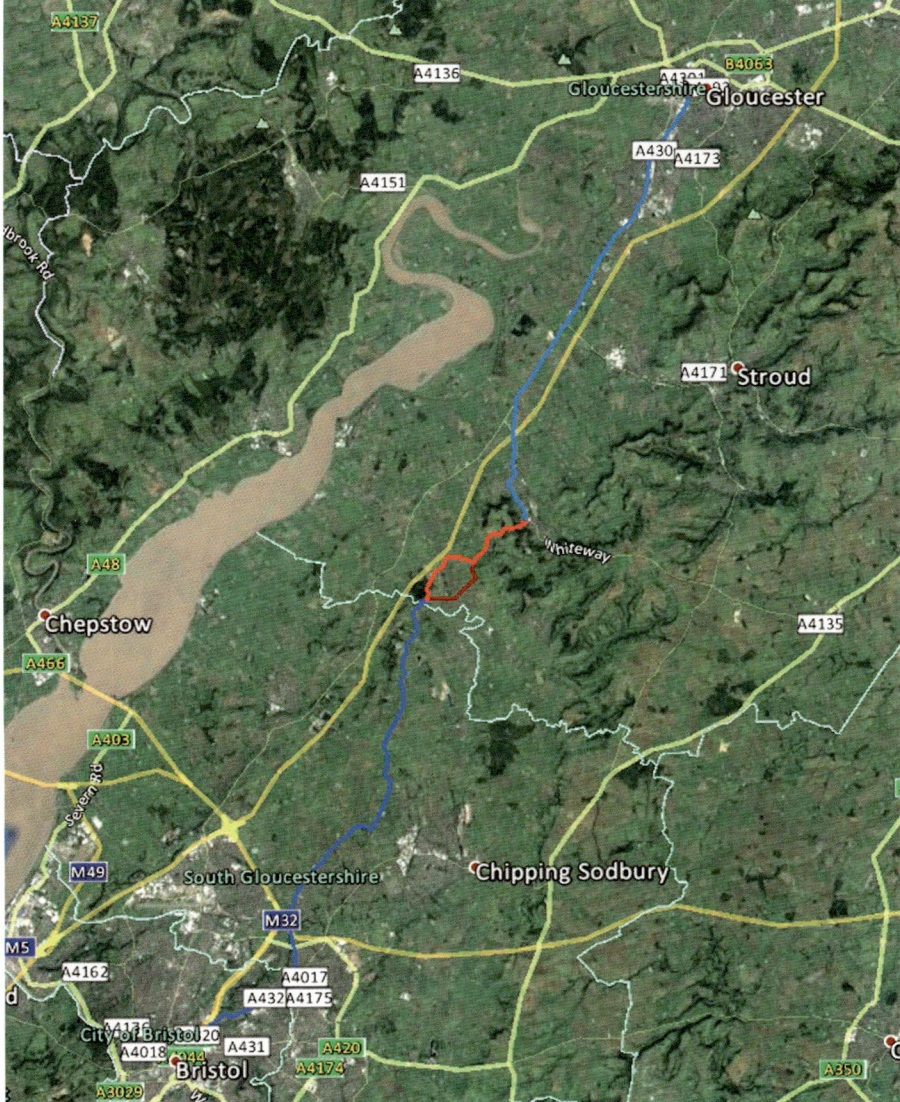

The same route superimposed on GEP with the known parts in blue and guessed parts in red.

as normal in the 16th century that if a road was blocked, traffic would simply make its way over land adjoining it which of course was a menace to agriculture.

The government of the day therefore tried to do something about it. They decreed in an Act in 1555 (amended in 1563 and again in 1575 because it was not working) that the parish was responsible for the roads that ran through it. Parishioners were required to spend a given number of days per year working on their roads and a parish surveyor was appointed to oversee the repairs. While this might seem a good idea, in practice it did not work very well. The surveyor's position

Changes 1500 – 1700 • 45

A painting of a typical coaching scene in Bedale, North Yorkshire.

The same scene today. (CC)

was unpaid and his workers, many of whom may not even have used the roads, were reluctant and not too bothered about doing a decent job. On top of this, the parish could be fined and many were. Some parishes were less populated than others or had more miles of road or more heavily used roads and consequently struggled. For example, the parish of Standon in Hertfordshire had four miles of the Great North Road to deal with and was regularly hauled up at the Quarter sessions for defaulting. The problems appear to have been the weather,

Village street in Dunster, Somerset.

The same scene today. (GEP)

undergrowth, and the lack of decent methods of repair. Drainage was the biggest problem but until better methods were invented, there was not a huge amount that could be done.

The real argument centred around who should pay for the upkeep of roads, the folks that used it, the local parishes through which they ran, or the country in general. The next step was to try and charge the road user and this gave rise to the turnpiking era.

TURNPIKING AND THE COACHING ERA

WILLIAM STOUT, BORN IN 1665 was a wholesale grocer and ironmonger based in Lancaster and being an educated man he kept a diary which was later published as an autobiography. While a lot of it is concerned with accounts, home life and personal affairs, some of it details his travels. He did quite a lot of travelling, mostly to do with his business including going to such places as Nottingham, Leicester, Sheffield and London, where he went at least once a year. Clearly from his writings he did this on horseback rather than in a coach. He also mentions the problems with the transport of his merchandise and raw materials. Between 1688 and 1714, England was (as usual) at war with France excepting a break between 1697 and 1701. Stout notes that the French privateers at sea were disrupting trade to such a degree that they were turning to overland transport which was more expensive. Road transport was usually kept locally, for example to markets or to the nearest ports. Thus, up to this point England's freight transport system was very much water based. However, the waterways were also finding it hard to cope with ever increasing demand. Weather again played a part with ice, floods or droughts creating problems and weirs or mills blocked waterways. Ports silted up and docks were not always maintained. The ongoing wars drew seamen away to the Navy and ships and cargos were lost or taken. This could create major delays in the transport of goods and the prices rose accordingly. Clearly something had to change.

We left our road system being cared for by the parishes through which they ran. However, in some places, local people with an interest in transporting goods got together and petitioned parliament for the authority to take on a particular project. Both on land and on water these improvement projects often met with opposition. From groups who already had some interest in transport in that area who feared losing revenue to the new project or from landowners or farmers. These disputes were country wide but it is clear that slowly the improvers were winning the battle as the number of improvement acts grew steadily in the early 1700s.

Broadfield toll bar, Abbeydale Road, Sheffield. Painting by William Highfield around 1900. The toll bar closed in 1873.

The same place today, from country lane to busy city street. (GEP)

The principle that travellers should contribute to the upkeep to road improvement was first embodied in a turnpike authority act in 1663 on the Great North Road in Hertfordshire. This was a temporary measure to provide money to maintain a particularly troublesome section of the Great North Road. This had been attempted earlier in the 17th century but defeated in parliament. The parish mentioned in the last chapter, Standon in Hertfordshire appears to be behind the 1663 Act. It had four hilly miles of the Great North Road to administer,

Heeley Toll Bar, Chesterfield Road, Sheffield. Also by William Highfield.

The same spot today. (GEP)

which were heavily used by wagons taking malt to Ware and being only a small parish was struggling to fulfil its duties. After being taken to the assizes on a number of occasions for defaulting they petitioned parliament for assistance on more than one occasion and suggested taxing the heavy wagons using the road. Joined by a couple of adjoining parishes they finally succeeded with the 1663 Act. This was clearly only meant to be a temporary toll for a special case and not an attempt to create a new system of road improvement. As such the parish was still responsible for the upkeep but was allowed to exact a toll to finance the repairs. Also, around this time each county appointed surveyors who supervised roads in the entire county. They allowed toll gates to be set up at Wadesmill, Stilton and Caxton on the Great North Road. It is not clear exactly how long these gates lasted as there was much local opposition and no more turnpike Acts were passed for at least 30 years.

However, traffic was still increasing becoming more acute because of the war mentioned by William Stout and the ensuing disruption of coastal shipping. From 1695 to 1706 several new Acts were passed giving justices the power to erect gates and collect tolls. And then a new Act was passed. In 1706 instead of the local justices or parishes, a board of trustees was given same powers as the justices dealing with a stretch of road between Stoney Stratford and Fornhill in Buckinghamshire. I suspect that Fornhill is where Fourne Hill farm stands just north of Hockliffe, so the stretch in question was a major road on the line of Roman Watling Street (current A5). The trustees were authorised to erect gates, collect tolls, appoint surveyors and demand labour. By 1714 these types of Turnpike Trust had completely replaced the earlier justice-controlled trusts possibly because of the other commitments of justices getting in the way of their effective administration. The relationship between parish and road repair was now almost totally severed.

Groups of local residents would get together to form and fund a Turnpike Trust and a petition would be drawn up, given to the local MP and read out in parliament. The case was looked into by a committee and if found to be viable then the Act was passed. The people who grouped together were town councils, farmers, businessmen and manufacturers, landowners or traders. In other words, anyone who had an interest in having a decent transport system. It is clear however that resistance to toll roads was not going away as there was much opposition to the new road authorities. Accusations abounded, particularly that stretches were allowed to fall into decay so that a Trust might be obtained to transfer costs to road users or that only a small part of the proposed Turnpike needed repair. Also, there was competition between Trusts who did not want nearby rival turnpikes being established and taking their business. There was additionally a class element, the improvements were seen as favouring coach traffic more than wagon and horse traffic which were used by the general populace.

As well as local and parliamentary opposition there were more violent protests. Rioting occurred all over England and tollgates were destroyed and toll collectors assaulted. The penalties for such action rose swiftly from fines, imprisonment or whipping to transportation or the death penalty over a period of 30 years from around 1725. After major riots in the Bristol area on a number of occasions between 1727 and 1749 and in Leeds in 1753 this seemed to settle down until the so called Rebecca riots in the 1830s. Men dressed as women and calling themselves 'Rebecca and her Daughters', believed to be an Old Testament reference, started tearing gates down again in an area in Wales. It should be mentioned that the road tolls were not the only social problem at the time and a general poverty was the main cause of unrest.

Over a period then of around 150 years from 1700 to 1850 many turnpike trusts were established from a slow beginning and as they gained acceptance the opposition waned and more trusts were established over time.

We should not imagine a logical progression of turnpike roads, rather they sprang up here and there, slowly grew and eventually joined up. We cannot say that a road we know well today as one entity

A Punch cartoon of the era showing rioters dressed as women tearing down a toll gate.

Another illustration from the Illustrated London News in 1843. Once again showing rioters dressed as women tearing down a toll gate.

was turnpiked in one go. As an example, the dates and distances covered of the Turnpike Acts for the Great North Road in England are as follows (from *Albert, Appendix C*)

Islington – Highgate	4 miles	1717
Highgate – Barnet	6 miles	1711
Barnet – Gally Corner	1 mile	not turnpiked
Gally Corner – Lemsford	9 miles	1730
Lemsford – Stevenage	7 miles	1726
Stevenage – Biggleswade	12 miles	1720
Biggleswade – Alconbury	22 miles	1725

(The stretch between Alconbury and Wansford was covered by the Royston and Wansford Turnpike Trust)

Wansford – Stamford	6 miles	1749
Stamford – Grantham	22 miles	1739
Grantham – Drayton	28 miles	1726
Drayton – Bawtry	14 miles	1766
Bawtry – Doncaster	8 miles	1776
Doncaster – Boro'bridge	42 miles	1741
Boroughbridge – Durham	48 miles	1745
Durham – Newcastle	14 miles	1747
Newcastle – Buckton	51 miles	1747
Buckton – Berwick	10 miles	1753

Turnpiking and the Coaching Era

Pitsmoor Toll Bar, Barnsley Road, Sheffield. Another painting by William Highfield.

The same place today and the building still stands! (GEP)

A total then of 304 miles over 40 years. Eventually most of the main road network was turnpiked and to this day milestones can be seen on older stretches of road bearing the name of the turnpike trust which placed it there. Another consequence of this period was that a number of engineers made names for themselves as they were employed to improve bridges, tunnels, road surfaces and drainage. Telford, Brunel and McAdam are names we all know 200 years on.

One thing which may still be seen today are the toll houses. The gates are long gone but many of the small houses built for the toll keepers still exist. They often have a round or even octagonal section believed to be so that the keepers could see the roads in all directions.

Copeland in his *Roads and their Traffic 1750 – 1850* records some of the accounts from turnpike trusts which make for interesting reading.

This is the Toll gate traffic return for the first week of April 1823 for the various gates operated by the Bath Trust

Carriage of stone	
6" wagons	72
6" carts	66
Narrow wagons	58
Narrow carts	17
Carriage of coal	
6" wagons	108
6" carts	243
Narrow wagons	96
Narrow carts	435
Carriage of sundries	
9" wagons	37
6" wagons	114
6" carts	147
Narrow wagons	128
Narrow carts	425
Light carts	665
Carriages with four wheels	
4 horse	39
2 horse	583
1 horse	55
Stagecoaches	
4 horse	240
2 horse	157
Sheep (score)	73
Cattle (score)	12¾
Saddle horses	3634
Gigs	483

Noticeably the single horse is by far the most common mode of transport even at this date. The post coach is not mentioned as they were free from tolls. The reference to 9" and 6" wagons refer to the

Shackerley Toll Bar, Preston New Road, Mellor, Lancs. A painting by Henry Crossland date unknown.

The same stretch of road today, according to an old map, the toll bar stood right here. (GEP)

width of the wheels. Heavy wagons were making a real mess of the roads and so parliament allowed wagons with broader wheels to go cheaper on the turnpikes, with a corresponding raise for wagons with narrower wheels. Needless to say, this was not universally popular!

Another table shows the quarterly amounts raised at the Shenfield tollgate, just outside Brentwood in Essex on the main road to London from Chelmsford, Colchester and Ipswich.

Year	Jan-Mar	Apr-Jun	Jul-Sept	Oct-Dec	Yearly Total
1819	488.14.0	515.10.2	512.0.0	467.3.3	£1,983.7.4
1824	470.2.0	463.0.3	458.9.3	483.15.9	£1,875.7.3
1830	418.12.6	462.18.6	416.18.0	424.18.0	£1,723.7.0

The amounts are in old style monetary notation before decimalisation. Thus £.s.d where s = shillings and d = pence. So 488.14.0 is 488 pounds, 14 shillings and 0 pence. There were 12 pence in a shilling and 20 shillings in a pound.

It is interesting to note that over the year the amounts stay fairly constant which may be because of the traffic to London. Other areas would probably have had more seasonal variation.

There were of course expenses too. By far the largest was the upkeep of the road, materials and repairs to road furniture coming in a close second.

One extra thing was that turnpike trusts were required by law to have a milestone at every mile. They usually had the turnpike trust's name on and can still be seen dotted all over the country.

All in all, the Turnpiking era without a doubt helped to provide a backbone of reasonable roads. Turnpike trusts were not ideal, often inefficient, and occasionally dishonest. Macadam who became

Another toll house in the Sheffield area. Believed to be on the Sheffield and Tinsley Trust route. So somewhere on present day Attercliffe Road. I was not able to find it on an old map. Note the tram lines. I wonder if the industry in the background is the Park Gate iron and steel works?

Typical turnpike trust milestones. Note they carry the name of the trust on them. (CC)

'Surveyor general of Metropolitan roads' in 1820 often complained that the turnpike trusts were too small, too localised to be efficient. It should also be mentioned that only around 20% of the country's roads were turnpiked and the rest were not much better than before. Even in 1850 complaints were still being made about cross-country roads.

Concurrent with the slow improvements in turnpikes and road surfaces, the coach as a method of long distance travel was also gaining popularity. Coachbuilding had improved and there were now vehicles available which could take advantage of better road surfaces. A rudimentary service had existed from around the turn of the 17th century and by the 1750s

A toll gate in Widemarsh Street Hereford.

According to an old map, the gate stood right here.
(GEP)

speeds were up at the heady heights of 10mph. This may seem paltry by today's standards, but it was a huge improvement at the time. Bulky goods still generally went by water which was very slow but people and more importantly mail could now travel across the country with journey times measured in hours in some cases rather than days!

It is strange to realise in our days of smartphones, Facebook Messenger, Whats App and email but you couldn't contact anybody who lived any distance away without sending a physical message.

Turnpiking and the Coaching Era • 59

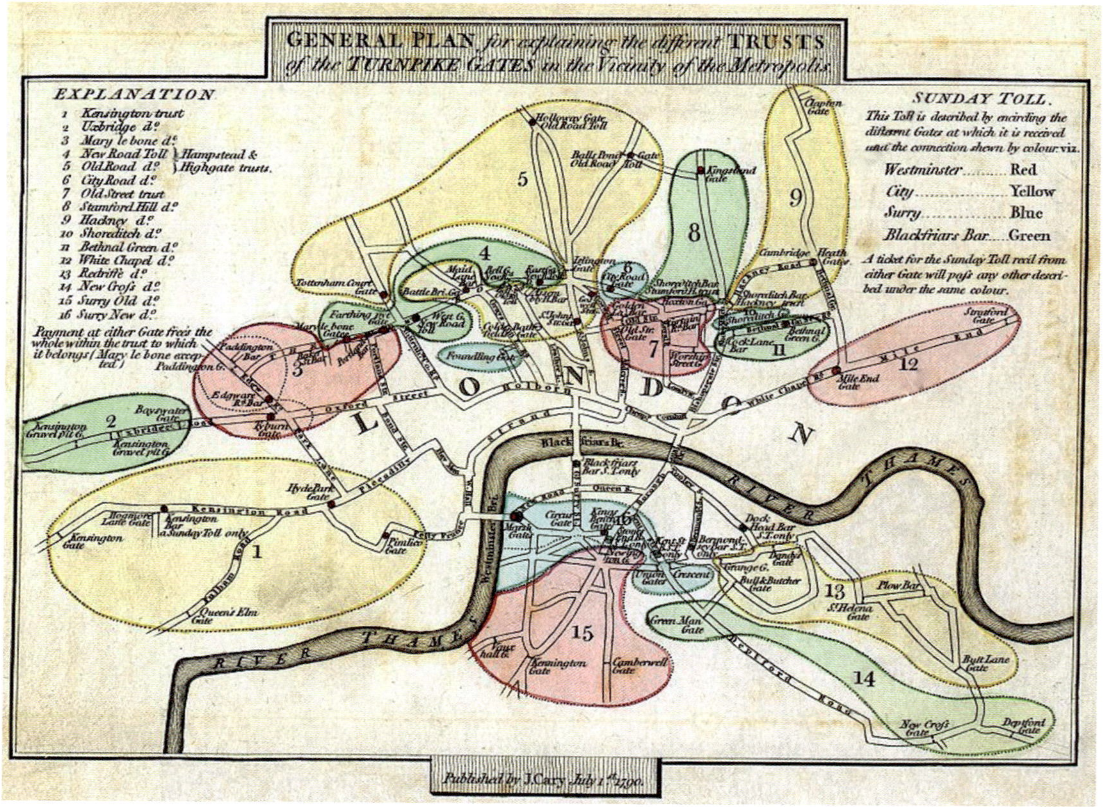

A map by John Cary of the turnpike trusts of London.

An engraving showing the Archway Road in north London. The toll gate is clearly visible as is the old bridge which gave Archway Road its name.

This included the government who of course had a great interest in sending and receiving messages as quickly as possible. To this end Henry VIII appointed a 'Master of the Posts', a title later changed to 'Postmaster General' which continues to this day.

An early photograph of a coach standing outside York Minster. Judging by its size and the single horse, it was probably a private coach..

From the 1600s up until this point, mail had been carried by 'post boys' men who rode horses from one end of the kingdom to the other, changing them regularly and delivering mail to postmasters. This was prone to robbery and inefficiency and eventually in 1782 a Bath man called John Palmer noted that the stagecoach between London and Bath took less time than the mail. He suggested a coach service that carried the mails and did not stop except to change horses. He arranged a trial run in 1785 which ran from Bristol to London in 16 hours, a great improvement. Thus, the Post Coach was born. It was a government monopoly and subject to a number of regulations. It was free from turnpike tolls and only stopped long enough to change the horses. The coach, the driver and the horses were all contracted out to the best tender and the coach carried a Royal Mail guard who had a sealed timepiece and a horn as well as weapons. He had to get tickets signed at the delivery points to prove that they had run on time and the horn was used to warn tollgate keepers and other road users

Painting by Samuel Alken around 1850 showing a typical stagecoach outside the Five Bells in New Cross. Looks to be quite busy too!

The Five Bells still stands on the A2 in south east London. (GEP)

that the mail was coming through. They had priority and the gates were supposed to be open by the time the coach arrived and other road users were supposed to give way.

Concurrently with the post coaches, stage coaching was becoming big business. Much like the post coaches, the hardware was all contracted out. Coach builders leased their vehicles to operators

A painting by James Pollard showing the Tally Ho London to Birmingham coach on the Great North Road in Highgate. The building in the background is Whittington college almshouses which stood from 1824 to 1967 when they were demolished to make way for the widening of the Archway Road.

The same place today. (GEP)

Turnpiking and the Coaching Era

much in the same way that today's railway locomotives are generally leased to the operators. Coaching inns vied for the trade providing horses for changes and fare for passengers. Operators painted their coaches in liveries much like today's bus companies. In fact, you might be surprised as to how familiar they might look. Destination signs, advertisements and company logos were all the rage. The contracts provided a regular income for some large operations and some astute businessmen made a fortune.

Men such as William Chaplin (1787-1859) who owned the Swan with Two Necks in Lad Lane (now Gresham Street) near St Pauls and very close to the Post Office buildings, the Spread Eagle in Gracechurch Street, the White Horse in Fetter Lane and possibly others all of

A painting by George Wright showing a stage coach outside the Bell inn at Stilton on the Great North Road. The inn's ornate wrought iron sign is visible.

Another inn which still stands along with its ornate sign. This road however goes nowhere now, it was bypassed by the A1(M) and is in fact a dead end. (GEP)

The 'Comet' and the 'Highflyer' pass each other at some speed. Artist and location unknown.

which had coach departures. Clearly an astute businessman he also owned large herds of horses and employed a large number of staff. It was massive business of the time. By the turn of the 18th century, the so called 'Golden Age of Coaching' had begun.

John Cary was a London engraver who was well known for his maps and atlases. In 1794 he was commissioned by the Postmaster General to survey England's roads. The result of this was Cary's New Itinerary, an atlas of the main roads of the country. Cary went further, his itinerary not only catalogued all the main roads of the country but described how to get practically anywhere by coach. A 'coach timetable' if you like. I managed to get a facsimile copy of this so let us see if I can get home from London using this 1798 work.

The first part lists all the places on the direct roads from London and the second part, many other places in the country and their relationship to the nearest place on the main roads. I live near Hovingham in North Yorkshire which is most definitely not on a main road so it does not show up in the first list of places. It is however in the second list; its entry reads as follows . . .

Hovingham Yorks.N 8 L New Malton 495

This is deciphered thus, Hovingham in North Yorkshire 8 miles off to the left from New Malton (as it was then known) and the road upon which you find Malton is on page 495. So, we go to page 495 to find that Malton is on the route of a provincial mail coach from York to Whitby. York appears on the list of places that can be reached direct from London. Looking up York in the list of places reached from London gives us a list of 10 coaches we can choose from to go to York.

66 • HIGHWAYS OF BRITAIN – Then and Now

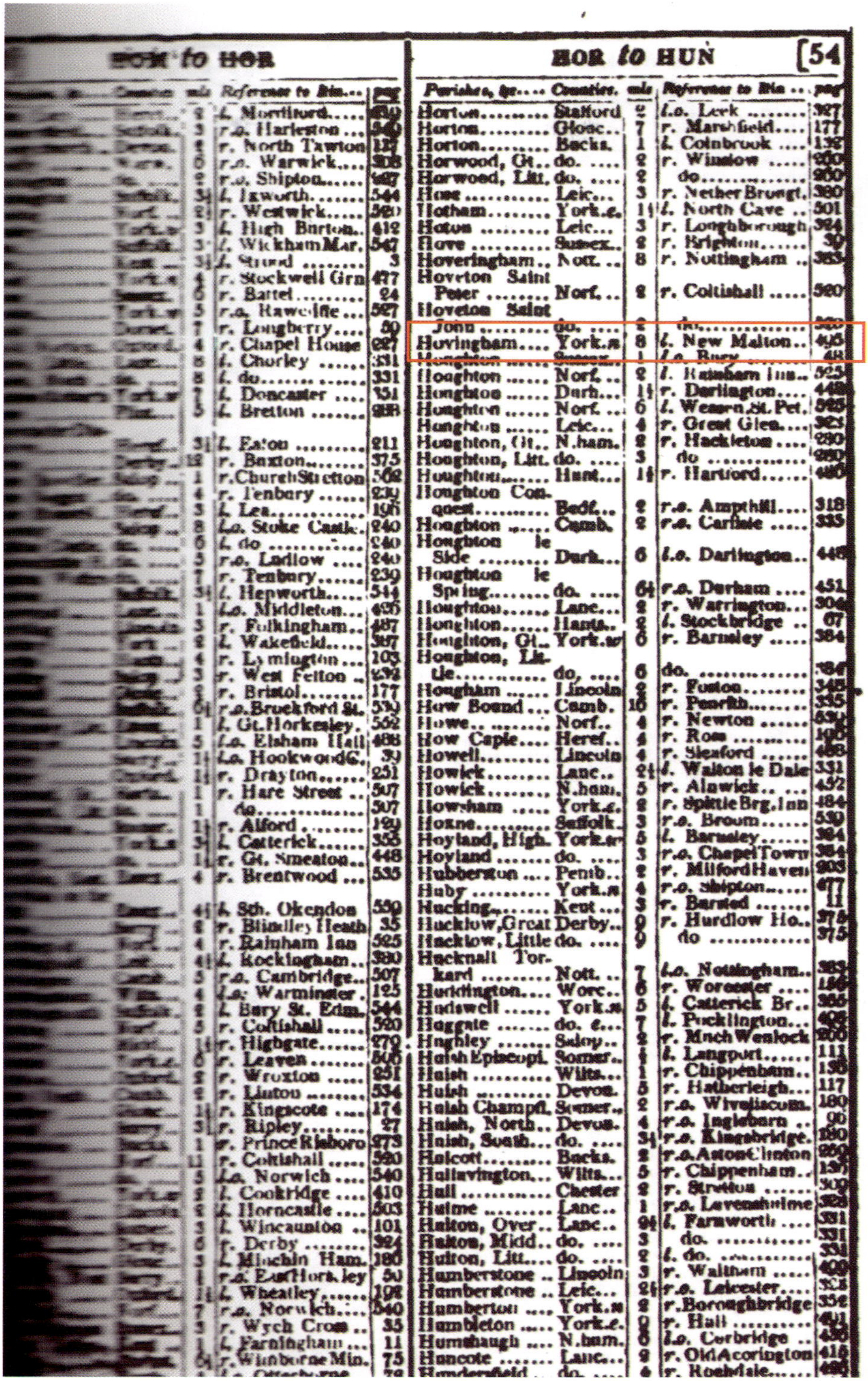

HOR to HOR				HOR to HUN				[54
	mls	Reference to Itin...	pag	Parishes, &c...	Counties	mls	Reference to Itin...	pag
	2	L. Mortiford...		Horton	Stafford	2	L.o. Leek	127
	3	r.o. Harleston	540	Horton	Glouc.	7	r. Marshfield	177
	4	r. North Tawton	127	Horton	Bucks	1	L. Colnbrook	132
	6	r.o. Warwick	208	Horwood, Gt.	do.	2	r. Winslow	200
	2	r.o. Shipton	127	Horwood, Litt.	do.	2	do	200
	3½	L. Ixworth	544	Hose	Leic.	3	r. Nether Brought.	380
	2	r. Westwick	520	Hotham	York.e.	11½	r. North Cave	501
	3	L. High Burton	412	Hoton	Leic.	3	r. Loughborough	324
	3	r. Wickham Mar.	547	Hove	Sussex	2	r. Brighton	30
	3½	L. Strood	3	Hoveringham	Nott.	8	r. Nottingham	353
	4	r. Stockwell Grn	477	Hoveton Saint Peter	Norf.	2	r. Coltishall	520
	6	L. Battel	24	Hoveton Saint John	do.	2		
	5	r.o. Rawcliffe	527	**Hovingham**	**York.**	**8**	**L. New Malton**	**495**
	1	r. Longberry	50	Houghton	Norf.	2	L. Rainham Inn	525
	4	Chapel House	227	Houghton	Durh.	1½	r. Darlington	445
	5	L. Chorley	331	Houghton	Norf.	6	L. Western St. Pet.	525
	8	L. do	331	Houghton	Leic.	4	r. Great Glen	323
	7	L. Doncaster	151	Houghton, Gt.	N.ham.	2	r. Hackleton	290
	5	L. Bretton	388	Houghton, Litt.	do.	3	do	290
	3½	L. Eaton	211	Houghton	Hunt.	1½	r. Hartford	480
	12	r. Buxton	575	Houghton Conquest	Beds.	2	r.o. Ampthill	318
	1	L. Churchstretton	562	Houghton	Camb.	2	r. Carlisle	335
	4	r. Tenbury	239	Houghton le Side	Durh.	6	L.o. Darlington	445
	1	L. Lea	195	Houghton le Spring	do.	6½	r.o. Durham	451
	8	L.o. Stoke Castle	240	Houghton	Lanc.	2	r. Warrington	306
	6	L. do	240	Houghton	Hants.	2	L. Stockbridge	67
	2	r.o. Ludlow	240	Houghton, Gt.	York.w	6	r. Barnsley	384
	1	r. Tenbury	239	Houghton, Lit.	do.		do	384
	3½	L. Hepworth	544	Hougham	Lincoln	6	r. Foston	345
	3	L.o. Middleton	425	How Bound	Camb.	10	r. Penrith	335
	5	r. Folkingham	487	Howe	Norf.	4	r. Newton	539
	4	L. Wakefield	387	How Caple	Heref.	4	r. Ross	195
	4	r. Lymington	103	Howell	Lincoln		r. Sleaford	468
	2	r. West Felton	498	Howick	Lanc.	2½	L. Walton le Dale	331
	2	r. Bristol	177	Howick	N.ham.	1	r. Alnwick	452
	2	r.o. Brockford	539	Howsham	York.e.	2	r. Spittle Brg. Inn	484
	1	L. Gt. Horkesley	562	Hoxne	Suffolk	3	r.o. Broom	539
	2	L.o. Elsham Hall	488	Hoyland, High.	York.w	3	L. Barnsley	384
	1½	L.o. Hookwood G.	79	Hoyland	do.	3	r.o. Chapeltown	384
	1	r. Drayton	251	Hubberston	Pemb.	4	r.o. Milford Haven	503
	2	r. Hare Street	507	Huby	York.n	2	r.o. Shipton	477
	1	do	507	Hucking	Kent	3	r. Barnet	
	2	r. Alford	199	Hucklow, Great	Derby	2	r. Hurdlow Ho.	375
	3½	L. Catterick	353	Hucklow, Little	do.	2	do	375
	1	r. Gt. Smeaton	448	Hucknall Torkard	Nott.	7	L.o. Nottingham	353
	4	r. Brentwood	535	Huddington	Worc.	5	r. Worcester	186
	4½	L. Sch. Okendon	550	Hudswell	York.n	5	L. Catterick Br.	353
	2	r. Blindley Heath	35	Haggate	do. e.	7	L. Pocklington	408
	2	r. Rainham Inn	525	Hughley	Salop	2	r. Much Wenlock	200
	4½	L. Rockingham	390	Huish Episcopi	Somer.	1	L. Langport	111
	3	r. Cambridge	507	Huish	Wilts.	5	r. Chippenham	136
	2	L.o. Warminster	125	Huish	Devon	5	r. Hatherleigh	117
	2	L. Bury St. Edm.	544	Huish Champfl.	Somer.	2	r.o. Wiveliscomb	180
	2	r. Coltishall	520	Huish, North	Devon	4	r.o. Ingleborn	90
	1½	r. Highgate	270	Huish, South	do.	3½	r.o. Kingsbridge	180
	2	r. Leaven	506	Halcott	Bucks	2	r.o. Aston Clinton	259
	2	r. Wroxton	251	Hullavington	Wilts.	5	r. Chippenham	137
	2	r. Linton	534	Hull	Chester	2	r. Stretton	309
	3½	r. Kingscote	174	Hulme	Lanc.	1	r.o. Levenshulme	331
	3	r. Ripley	27	Hulton, Over	Lanc.	9½	L. Farnworth	331
	1	r. Prince Risboro	273	Hulton, Midd.	do.	2	do	331
	4	L.o. Coltishall	520	Hulton, Litt.	do.	2	do	
	5	L.o. Norwich	540	Humberstone	Lincoln	3	r. Waltham	409
	2	L. Cookridge	410	Humberstone	Leic.	2	r. Leicester	323
	2	L. Horncastle	503	Humberton	York.n	2	r. Boroughbridge	352
	2	L. Wincanton	101	Hambleton	York.e.	8	r. Hull	441
	1	r. Derby	324	Hambaugh	N.ham.	2	r. Corbridge	439
	3	L. Minchin Ham.	190	Huncote	Lanc.	2	r. Old Accrington	416
	1	r.o. East Horsley	50	Huddersfield			r. Rochdale	490
	1½	L. Wheatley	198					
	1	r.o. Norwich	540					
	1	r. Wych Cross	35					
	2	L. Farningham	11					
	1	L. Wimborne Min.	75					
		Otterbourne	70					

The page in Cary's Itinerary showing Hovinghams entry.

The entry for New Malton in the itinerary, note the names of the inns in between York and Malton.

495]　　Roads measured from Shoreditch Church.

To Whitby.	M	F	M	F
To ⌘ᵖYORK*, *as p.* 476			195	1
Lobster Inn*	7	5	202	6
Spittle Bridge Inn*	3	1	205	7
Whitwell Inn*	1	4	207	3
ᵇᵖNEW MALTON*—— *White Horse* 763 *H.* 3713 *I.*—Ma. ar. 3-40 Mo.; dep. 6 Aft. *On r. to Scarboro*, 22½ M.	5	4	212	7
Old Malton—*Church*	1	–	213	7
Cross the Rye R. whose Course on r. is to the Derwent R.				
ᵖPICKERING*—*Cross* 540 *H.* 2332 *I.*	7	5	221	4
Saltersgate Inn	8	2	229	6
Sleights*—*R. Lion Inn*	8	4	238	2
Cross the Esk R. whose Course on r. is to the Sea at Whitby.				
Ruswarp*——*Admiral Rodney Inn*	2	1	240	3
ᵖWHITBY*—*Drawbridge* 1393 *H.* 6969 *I.*—Ma. ar. 9 Mo.; dep. 1 Aft.	2	1	242	4

　　INNS. Whitwell, *Bay Horse.* Castle Howard Park *Inn.* New Malton, *W. Horse, Talbot.* Pickering, *Black Swan, W. Swan.* Saltersgate, *Cart & Horses, Ship.* Whitby, *Angel, Golden Lion, King's Head, W. Horse.*

　　York *and* Lobster Inn, *between, on r. at* Stockton, Brockfield, Benjamin Agar, Esq.; *and* Sand Hutton, Rev. T. C. R. Read.

　　Spittle Bridge, 2 M. *on r. of, is* Howsham, Chas. Cholmeley, Esq.; *and* 2 M. *on l.* Sheriff Hutton Park, G. L. Thompson, Esq.

　　Whitwell, *on l. of,* Wm. Slee, Esq.

　　Between *Whitwell and* New Malton, *on the l. is* Castle Howard, Earl of Carlisle; *on r. is* Hutton Lodge, J. Parkhurst, Esq.

　　Old Malton, *at,* Malton Abbey, W. Wood Watson, Esq.

　　Pickering, 3 M. *before, on l.* Misperton Hall, Rev. F. W. Blomberg.

　　Pickering, *at,* Pickering Hall, Rev. A. Cayley; *on the r. of,* Thornton House, Richard Hill, Esq.

　　2 M. from *Pickering, on r.* thorp, — Fothergill, Esq.

Sleights, *at, on the l. is* Esk Campion Coates, Esq.

Between *Sleights and Ruswarp* are The Woodlands, — Esq.; *and* Car Hall, Mrs.

Ruswarp, *at,* — Ward, Esq

Between *Ruswarp and Whitby* is Airy Hill, R. Moorsom, Esq.

Whitby, *a little before, on l.* Castle, Jas. Wilson, Esq.

Near *Whitby see* Lark Hall, Esq.

Whitby *is a Town of high Antiquity and carries on a great Trade.*

At *Whitby, the Abbey, the Property of* Chas. Cholmeley, Esq.

About 3 M. *on l. of* Whitby grave Castle, Earl of Mulgrave.

To Helmesley *and* Kirby Moorside.		
To ⌘ᵖYORK, *as p.* 476		
Kettlestring		2
Sutton on the Forest*		5
Stillington*		
ᵖGilling*		
Oswaldkirk*		
Sproxton		
Cross the Rye R. (see p.-495)		
ᵖHELMESLEY* 263 *H.* 1415 *I.*—Ma. ar. 5 Mo.; dep. 2¼ Aft.		1
Nawton*		2
ᵖKIRBY MOORSIDE* 321 *H.* 1673 *I.*		3

　　INNS. Helmesley, *Bl. S ... cise Office.* Kirby Moorside,

　　Sutton on the Forest, *at, on* Hoar Harland.

　　Stillington, *at,* Stephen Cr...

　　Between *Stillington and* Gil... is Bransby, Fras. Cholme...

　　Gilling, *at, on l. is* Gilling ... G. Fairfax, Esq.; *near* 5 M... which is Newborough H... Wynn Belasyse, Esq.

　　Oswaldkirk, *at,* Rev. Mr. S...

　　Helmesley, *near, on l. is* D... Park, Charles Duncombe...

　　Nawton, 2 M. *beyond, on l*... House, Rev. John Robin...

68 • HIGHWAYS OF BRITAIN – THEN AND NOW

Index of Places in the Routes, &c.

Woodbridge, [378], 157, 165, 234, 349 M. 378
Woodford, [219, 717], 546
Woodford Bridge, 231
Woodstock, [55, 76, 788], 254 M.
Woolwich, [308]
Worcester
—by High Wycombe, [164, 191, 269 M. 270, 271, 347, 421, 494 M. 688, 787], 210, 239, 248, 253, 254 M. 410

Worcester
—by Henley, [28]
Worksop, 237
Wormley, 719
Worthing, [309, 348, 391, 495, 601, 646, 789, 790]
Wrexham, by Shrewsbury Coach
Wrotham, 116, 383, 384, 477, 650
Wycombe, High, [57, 68, 153], 42, 76, 104
Wymondham, 199, 259, 780

Yalding, [123, 392]
Yarm, 793
Yarmouth
—by Ipswich and Lowestoft, [349 M. 496 M. 553 M. 647, 791 M. 792]
Yeovil, 37 M. 40
York, [23, 29, 272 M. 350, 366, 422, 497, 587, 750, 793]
Yoxford, [165], 349 M. 496 N.

The entry for York indicating that there are 10 options to get there from London.

The itinerary is very much a book of lists which are cross referenced. Looking up the coach numbers for York we find

    York and Newcastle from the Angel Inn, Strand. Daily at 8.30am
    York from the Angel Inn, St Martins le Grand. Dep 6am
    York from the Bull and Mouth (a mail coach). Daily at 7.15pm
    York from the Cross Keys, Cheapside. Daily at 9am
    York from the Flower Pot, Bishopsgate. Daily at 9am
    York from the George and Blue Boar, Holborn. Daily at 6.45am
    York from the Golden Cross, Charing Cross. Dep 9am
    York from the Saracens Head, Snow Hill
    York from the White Bear, Piccadilly
    York from the White Horse, Fetter Lane

The fact that I have a choice of 10 coaches that go directly to York or pass through York illustrates clearly what big business this was. In 1798 I can get home to deepest North Yorkshire taking a coach from London to York, jumping on a mail coach to Whitby and getting out at Malton. Presumably the last 8 miles one either walked or took a horse or hackney carriage.

    As a matter of interest, I decided, as I am very familiar with the road between Malton and York to see if I could find the three inns mentioned in Cary as being on the coaching route. The Lobster Inn, the Spital Bridge Inn, and the Whitwell Inn. The Lobster is easy; it is still there although known as Lobster House Farm these days. It stands on a small ox bow stretch just off the modern A64 (see pics). The Spital

Bridge was a bit more difficult because I was misdirected by the fact that when I was a lad, there was a Spitalbeck Inn on the A64 just before Barton Hill. This building still stands although an Indian restaurant these days. However, a look on earlier maps showed no building on that site preceding the current one which appears to date to the 1930s. Now just north of this site there is a stretch of dual carriageway which has apparently been there since the mid-1930s according to the date stone on a railway bridge, although why they would build a stretch of dual carriageway on a fairly remote piece of road that long ago I do not know. The locals have been trying to get the rest of the A64 between York and Malton dualled for years as it gets very congested with holiday traffic heading for the North York Moors and the east coast. This dual carriageway leaves quite a long ox-bow stretch of old road off to one side. I had resigned myself to the fact the original Spital Bridge Inn must have been elsewhere and now demolished and lost to history. However, and somewhat embarrassingly, while I was working at a transport company sited on this ox-bow piece, I discovered that although the area comes under the name of the nearest village – Barton Hill – the beck that actually runs down one side of the freight yard is called the Spital beck. And if you walk about 50 yards up the oxbow stretch from our offices it goes under the old road which crosses on an old stone bridge which is called . . . you guessed it . . . the Spital Bridge! Just past this bridge is a small row of cottages and one of them is called 'The Old Spitalbeck'! So, I had another look at the old maps and sure enough in huge letters right where this cottage stands it says INN! Barely 200 yards from my office. Doh! As for the Whitwell Inn, it stands on the corner of Main Street and Tout Hill, although a private house now.

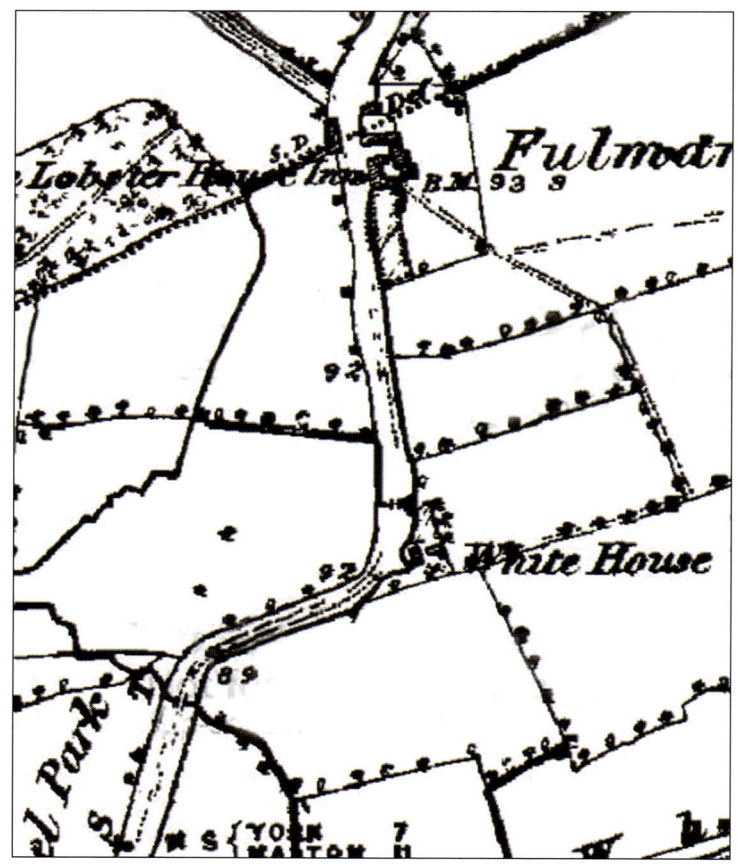

An 1853 map showing a kink in the road and the Lobster house inn.

An aerial view showing the kink has been ironed out and the Lobster house is still there as a farm. (GEP)

The Lobster House inn as was. (CC)

Turnpiking and the Coaching Era • 71

An aerial view of the A64 at Barton Hill showing the old road just north of the modern road, the Spital Bridge inn is in between the two industrial sites on the old road. (GEP)

The Old Spital Cottage once the Spital Bridge Inn.

A typical stretch of ox-bow road. Once the main road from York to Malton, now a backwater with a dual carriageway about 50 yards to the right. This is the old road shown in the overhead shot, now a dead end and unfortunately the full stretch can't be driven although both parts are accessible.

As far as our roads go though, the so called Golden Age of Coaching was brought to an abrupt halt by British engineers who had been trying to put steam engines on wheels.

John Maggs painted this view of a stage coach waiting to leave the Full Moon inn in Bath.

Both the inn and the old bridge are long gone, but this is the same place.
(GEP)

THE FALL AND RISE OF ROADS AND MODERN TIMES

BY THE MID 18TH CENTURY, the steam engine was being developed for use mainly in mines. They were originally developed as pumps but it was soon realised that they could have other uses and so different configurations of engines were soon being tried. Attempts were also being made to put steam engines on wheels. The problems faced by these attempts were many. The technology of the time favoured 'condensing' engines which were big, heavy and worked on a low steam pressure. Advances made by William Murdoch and Richard Trevithick in high pressure steam engines were opposed by James Watt and Matthew Boulton, the existing steam experts. However, some road vehicles were built and tested but other problems involving the suspension, braking and steering of such heavy vehicles also hampered progress. As did legislation. They were regarded as dangerous to other road users and to the road surfaces of the day. Tolls for road locomotives were punitive. Nobody liked a heavy vehicle on their road, a tradition that carries on to this day!

Railway locomotives however were another matter. I am guessing that railways were developed because mines already used trackways to transport their goods although the wagons were pulled by horses. In 1804 Richard Trevithick and a mine owner called Samuel Homfray mounted one of Homfrays mine engines onto wheels and to win a bet pulled 10 tons of iron ore ten miles along a mine railway between Merthyr Tydfil and Penydarren. This showed that railway transport was viable.

A number of further innovations allowed railway engines and iron rails to become commercially useful and in 1825 the famous Stockton and Darlington railway was built primarily to haul coal to the docks at Stockton. The success of this venture encouraged the building of the Liverpool and Manchester railway and the owners discovered that passengers wanted to use their railway too.

Railways exploded! Everyone wanted to get onto the bandwagon and local lines sprang up all over Britain. Interestingly to begin with, they developed very much in the same way as the turnpike road system did. Odd places all over the country connected with each other and started to join up, gradually being bought out and coalescing until by the time of the first world war there were 120 railway companies operating and often competing with each other. This was affecting revenues and efficiency so the newly formed Ministry of Transport created the Railways Act 1921 which grouped together the existing railway companies into 4 regional companies thus: – The London and North East Railway (LNER), The London, Midland and Scottish Railway (LMS), the Southern Railway (SR) and the Great Western Railway (GWR). The companies were huge concerns and owned not only trains and railways, but also hotels, ships and road vehicles. These 4 companies, known as the Big Four existed until nationalisation in 1948 when they were amalgamated to form British Rail.

So where does this leave our road system? Well, road use plummeted leaving many turnpike trusts and coaching companies in debt. The 'Golden Age of Coaching' ended abruptly. And everything that was not local traffic went by rail. Even small towns and villages had goods yards attached to their stations where goods were loaded or unloaded and distributed locally. Effectively road use went back to pre-turnpike levels. Goods went by rail. Stations had loading bays for specific commodities. I live only a couple of doors from what was the village railway station and the sidings area there was big enough to accommodate the caravan site which is there now. It had a goods shed, a three-storey grain loading shed, a cattle dock for loading or unloading cattle and of course the ever-present coal bins.

Between 1840 and 1870 the turnpike trusts declined at such a rate that in the 1870s the government felt that it was able to turn road control back over to local communities and trust renewals were no longer granted. In 1888 the Local Government Act created county councils and one of the duties given to the newly created councils was the maintenance of the county's roads. A number of events in the early 20th century however started to tip the balance back towards road use.

At the turn of the 20th century several engineers in both Europe and the USA were concurrently developing the internal combustion engine. Much lighter and smaller than the equivalent steam engines they were fitted to carriages to begin with and the motor car was born. Incidental to this were advances in mass production. Production lines in factories and the use of interchangeable parts allowed vehicles to be produced efficiently at a far greater rate than before, and more cheaply, thereby making them more accessible to the general public.

By 1910 there were around 140,000 road vehicles on the roads and the government took an interest creating a Road Board with powers to collect taxes off motorists the purpose of which was to upkeep the roads. It also had powers to acquire land on either side of highways to allow for widening, which it used very sparingly apparently. (From *British Highway Development before Motorways* by the RAC Foundation.)

World War I also contributed. Production lines went into high gear and developments happened quickly. By the end of that war the sale of surplus military trucks and other vehicles greatly accelerated the trend towards using them instead of railways, particularly for short journeys.

The Road Board only lasted 9 years (1910-1919) and was replaced by a new Ministry. The Ministry of Transport Act 1919 created a Ministry that had control over; railways; light railways; tramways; canals, waterways and inland navigations; harbours, docks and piers; roads, bridges and ferries and the vehicles and traffic thereon. The 'panel of experts' pertaining to roads was the Roads Advisory Committee which consisted of eleven members of which five were representatives of highway authorities and five were representative of the users of horse and mechanical road traffic and one representative of labour.

The newly formed Ministry of Transport changed the road taxation system and also;

Introduced a national system of road signage

Carried out the first national road traffic census in 1922

Introduced the highway code and compulsory third party insurance

Set up a research laboratory to investigate matters of road construction, design and safety

Introduced guidance and standards for a range of highway design and management topics (including street lighting, traffic signals and road safety)

Developed a national system of speed limits

Introduced the system of Traffic Commissioners

Introduced compulsory driving tests in 1935

Developed a main roads improvement programme – and saw the demise of the hypothecated road fund.

(From the RAC Foundation.)

At this time, the Ministry did not have direct control over the road system but had to work through and fund the county councils. This changed with the Trunk Roads Act of 1936 when the Ministry took direct control. During WWII the Ministry was temporarily replaced with the Ministry of War Transport. On that note apart from the removal of road signs and the blackout, I find no evidence that WWII had any direct effect on the roads system. The Ministry of War Transport was much more concerned with actual transport rather than the infrastructure. However, the Ministry of War Transport experience led directly to the nationalisation of Britain's transport system in 1947.

Going back to 1919, the ministry lost no time in classifying its road system and this is when road numbers came into being. This was done in 1922 and created numeric 'zones' divided by single digit A roads. The A1 through A6 run from London radially to various parts of England and Wales and the zone clockwise of each road is given its number. Thus, the area east of the A1 is the 1 zone, the area south and west of the A2 is the 2 zone and so on. The A7, A8 and A9 perform the same function based on Edinburgh. The one exception to this rule is that the part of Kent between the A2 and the Thames estuary is seen as being in the 2 zone.

Roads that are regarded as beginning in a particular zone are given its first digit. Larger, more important roads are given two-digit numbers eg; A27, A38, A92. These are known as the First 99 (or F99) amongst SABRE users. Lesser roads have three- or four-digit numbers. The higher the number is indicative of how far from the hub the road is. So, the A13 is a major road close to London while the A15 is a major road further from London but both are in the 1 zone. Likewise, the A127 or A135 were closer to London than the A169 or A184.

As roads have been built or re-classified over the years since 1922 this is not as clear cut as it once was. You will find roads that are out of zone or start in one and finish in another. For example, the A135 mentioned above used to connect Colchester and Harwich. The number was removed in a 1935 revision of road numbers and the designation A135 currently refers to a road on Teesside. The 1935 revision was because although blocks of numbers had been set aside for future road projects, the scale of them was more than anticipated and maps were becoming out of date almost before they were printed.

In the 1920s, high unemployment caused by the return of millions of fighting men to a country that was embracing mechanisation led to unemployment relief programmes which incorporated road building, particularly in the London area. Many trunk roads, bridges and bypasses were built in this way between 1920 and 1930. Including the so-called 'arterial roads'. These were high-capacity (for their time) urban roads connecting population centres and bypassing towns.

By the 1930s, road use was on an unprecedented and meteoric rise which continues to this day. Clearly improvements were required. The arterial roads were built wide and sometimes dualled, the first use of dualling in the UK (a dual carriageway is where there is more than a painted line separating the directions of travel, there may be one or more lanes on each side). Many of the roads that are entirely dualled today began life as sections of dual carriageway bypassing towns. These were later linked up with new dualling. Some roads were not actually dualled, but had three lanes with the centre one available for use by traffic on either side. This was a highly dangerous situation and the middle lane soon got the name 'suicide lane'. It was quite common at one time, I remember seeing them myself, but they have been phased out.

On that subject, we tend to think of road accidents as a modern-day phenomenon but in fact they have been around since there have been vehicles on the roads. Certainly, there was a fatal crash at Croxdale bridge on the Great North Road in County Durham in 1822 when a stagecoach crashed and passengers were thrown into the river. Other causes of coaching incidents included wheel collapse, faulty brakes and runaway horses. Also, as the coaches stopped every ten or twelve miles at a coaching inn, the drivers tended to imbibe more ale than was strictly good for them or their passengers!

In more recent times, Edwin Sewell a 31-year-old engineer and his passenger a Major Richer became the first recorded fatalities in a motor vehicle when they crashed a Daimler car after one of the wheels collapsed on Grove Hill in Harrow, London. Since then as we are sadly aware there have been thousands of deaths on our road system and it is not surprising that within the list of deaths there are some quite well-known names.

Major T E Lawrence aka Lawrence of Arabia was a keen motorcyclist and owned a number of Brough Superior SS100s, a very expensive hand-built motorcycle of the time. On 13 May 1935 he crashed between his home at Clouds Hill, Dorset and Bovington army camp. He died 6 days later. It is probable that a crash helmet would have saved his life.

Unsurprisingly, racing drivers like to drive fast and it would appear that this was the case when Mike Hawthorn, a well knownGrand Prix driver of the 1950s crashed his car on January 22nd 1959. The accident happened on a well-known accident blackspot on the Guildford bypass and contemporary Pathe newsreels show a badly smashed Jaguar. The accident took place about 300 yards the Guildford side of the junction of the A3 and Manor Way.

Two overhead views of the Mike Hawthorn crash site on the A3 near Guildford.

Musicians are also not exempt from death by road. Eddie Cochran, an up-and-coming musician and film star, was killed in a road accident in Chippenham, Wiltshire. He was in a taxi which crashed, killing him. The taxi driver was later prosecuted.

And perhaps the best known. Marc Bolan of T Rex. A popular figure and the man responsible for starting the Glam Rock era. He was killed in 1977 when a Mini driven by his girlfriend hit a tree on Queens Ride in South London. The site still has a shrine dedicated to him.

Lastly but not least Mike Hailwood was a well-known motorcycle racer who also had several forays into car racing. After retirement he opened a motorcycle dealership called Hailwood and Gould with a partner, ex motorcycle racer Rod Gould. I vaguely remember this shop as it was near my maternal grandparent's home in Birmingham and I had a developing love of motorcycling that continues to this day. Mike who lived in Tanworth in Arden was killed on the A435 in Portway, Warwickshire in 1981 sadly along with his 9-year-old daughter.

This small list of well-known road deaths is by no means complete and just scratches the surface of the depressingly large numbers of folk killed on the highways of Britain.

Many of these were single vehicle accidents but there have been some larger incidents with larger loss of life. An early one was the Dibbles Bridge coach crash where a coach had brake failure on 10 June 1925. It careered down a hill and through the parapet of a bridge over the River Dibb in North Yorkshire. 7 people were killed in what must have been a major incident at that time. Curiously almost exactly 50 years later another coach did the same thing and 33 people died. It is the worst accident by number of fatalities on British roads. This includes the occasional major motorway pile-up, for example the one that took place in fog on the M42 in March 1997. An initial collision in thick fog instigated what ended up as a 160-vehicle pile-up. While that sounds incredible, it's even more incredible that only 3 people died. This can probably be attributed to the safety advances in modern vehicle design which have reduced fatalities in accidents. I recall witnessing a head on collision in 1998 where a quite large modern car collided with a smaller older car. The larger car was totally spun round in the collision. On running over I discovered the occupants of the larger car unhurt. The smaller car driver died. While there is an element of size difference here, the larger car was equipped with up-to-date crumple zones and airbags, the smaller was not.

The table from the Department of Transport shows the numbers of fatalities on Great Britain's road since records began in 1926. It shows a remarkably high number of deaths in the 1920s considering the small

A photo taken at the time of the first Dibbles bridge coach crash in 1925.

The same place today. What isn't so visible is that in fact there is a house right behind me and this is someone's front yard. (CC)

amount of road traffic compared to today. The spike in 1941 represents the highest total during WWII. This is usually attributed to the blackout where all lights were extinguished or covered at night and car headlights were covered down to a slit. However, a study of the statistics shows that there were other considerations too. The rise in army and other

The Fall and Rise of Roads and Modern Times • 83

This graph from the Ministry of Transport clearly shows a decline in road deaths over time.

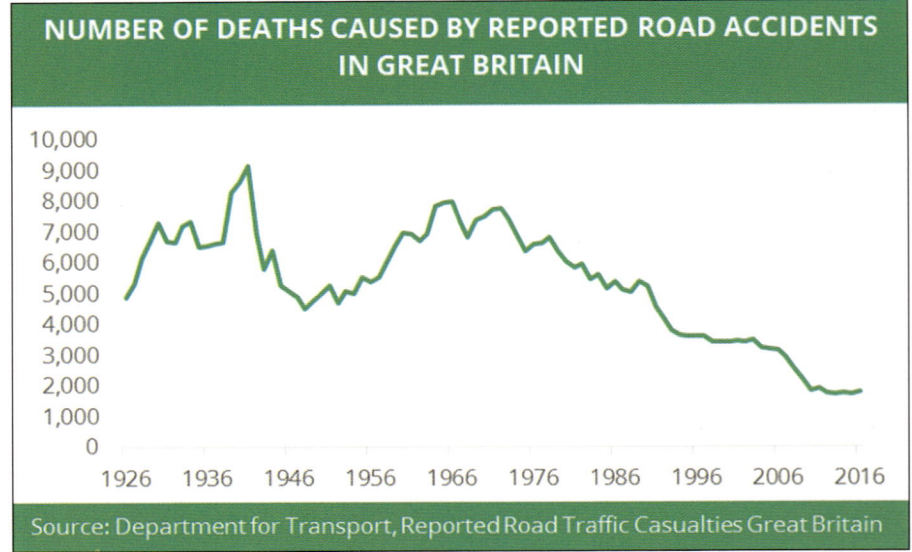

service vehicles is also believed to have had an impact. Child deaths rose during this time compared to pre-war and this is attributed to less supervision as parents were away at war or in munitions factories. By far the highest rise at this time though was among pedestrians in the winter months once again pointing to the dark being the major culprit.

Coming back to road expansion in the 1930s, Britain was lagging badly behind its European neighbours and the USA.

'Whilst little effort was made between the two world wars to establish a good quality national highway system in Britain much was being done in the United States, Italy and Germany. The first European motorway was constructed in northern Italy (Milan to Varese) in 1924 and by the outbreak of the Second World War the Germans had constructed over 3,300 kms of autobahn – not much less than the motorways we currently have in Britain almost seventy years later. The civil engineering capability this programme required must have been to Germany's advantage in the early years of the war. In the United States the first Parkways were introduced in 1926 and several major routes had been built by the end of the 1930s'.

(From *British Highway Development before Motorways* by the RAC Foundation.)

By the late 1930s, plans were in place to do something about this lack of infrastructure but WWII interceded and put any road building off until

This is Benwell Cross in Newcastle. Now this one had me foxed as I know this area and I know that St James' church is on the left of the road out of Newcastle centre.

I can only assume that this road at the back of the houses is the original road and that the current Adelaide Road was new built. (GEP)

This painting shows a typical un-metalled road at Kilton near Worksop in Nottinghamshire.

It has been altered slightly, but this is the same place. (CC)

the 1950s. In the late 1940s a number of plans were put forward but it was 10 years after the end of WWII before anything was actually done.

On December 5, 1958 a new bypass opened. This was the Preston bypass. It was a standard dual carriageway but this time there was a difference. Certain types of traffic were barred from using it and it was reserved solely for motorised transport. It was thus a 'motor way'. Prior to the Special Roads Act of 1949, any road immediately became a right-of-way open to any traffic, including horses and pedestrians. The Act barred certain classes of traffic from using them and no gas mains or sewage pipes nor anything else was allowed to be placed under them so they did not have to be dug up later (ha!). The motorway is the term used for such roads here but it is the legislation that sets them apart rather than any particular type of road. They are generally 2 or 3 lane dual carriageways (D2 or D3 classification) with motorway status (D2M or D3M). No side roads were allowed with access limited to junctions at set places.

As mentioned above, Britain was late to the motorway party, already in Europe, Italy and Germany had motorways, as did the USA. Some progress was made and some plans were put forward but not until after the dust from WWII settled was anything actually done. Eventually in the 1950s plans were put forward for a London to Yorkshire motorway, a West Midlands to Lancashire motorway, a West Midlands to the West Country motorway and a London to Wales motorway. These were finally approved and although built in stretches became the M1, M6, M5 and M4 respectively. Between 1958 and around 1978 the motorway system as we know it was pretty much constructed and although much more were planned, cuts and differing government views stifled many of those plans.

This shot shows the construction of Scammonden Bridge over the M62 to be.

This painting by Matthew Webb shows goods carts on a narrow and steep Newbury road in East Hendred Oxfordshire.

The current road is better surfaced, but still pretty narrow and steep. (GEP)

So, we have a sustained period of road building and improving from about the time the Ministry of Transport was ordained up until the present day with particular building surges in the 1920s and between around 1958-78. This has currently slowed although what has not slowed is car ownership or use. The existing roads are full now and apart from the current roll out of so-called smart motorways (a misnomer if there ever was one!) we are not doing much to address this problem. I do not know where the story will go from here.

STREET FURNITURE, ALTERATIONS AND OTHER INTERESTING THINGS

SO HOW DID OUR roads end up looking like they do today? Plastered in road signs and road markings, advertising, and furniture. Odd pieces of road orphaned in places. How do we make sense of what we see?

The earliest known use of road signs that we are aware of is the fingerpost. Common in Britain it simply consists of a post with arms (or fingers) on it pointing in the direction of a destination and usually included distanceinformation. While these were probably erected locally from an early time, there was legislation in the late 1600s that enabled magistrates to erect them at cross roads. Then, later on, the turnpike legislation actually required signage and milestones to be erected. Once the county councils took over the upkeep of their roads

Right and opposite: Typical Pre Warboys fingerposts near my home. (CC)

in the late 1800s it was they who were responsible for the signage. Many councils added the council's name to the sign. For example, there are still many fingerposts in North Yorkshire with a ring at the top of the post bearing the legend NRYCC (North Riding of Yorkshire County Council) or Yorkshire North Riding CC.

As far as other road signs go, they were initially used by cycling organizations in the 1880s who would put up 'danger boards' to warn cyclists of such things as crossroads, sharp bends or steep hills. These were adopted with the Motor Car Act of 1903 and consisted of a white post with a red triangle at the top. Some local authorities added a plaque detailing the hazard.

Street Furniture, Alterations and other Interesting Things • 91

One of the things the newly established ministry of transport did in the 1920s was to issue guidelines as to the colours, size and font used on road signs. These stayed in force until the The Traffic Signs (Size, Colour and Type) Provisional Regulations Act of 1933 established country wide specificationsand standardized the pictograms used on the warning signs.

However, only a short while later all signs in Britain were removed on the outbreak of WWII. Upon replacement in the late 1940s they were the same as before with the black and white poles and signs. Warning signs had red triangles at the top and regulatory signs had a red circle or disc. Things remained this way for a few more years until, in 1961, a graphic designer by the name of Herbert Spencer published two articles in his graphic art and design journal *Typographica*. These articles pointed out a number of shortcomings in the British road sign design. As a result, the government set up a committee to investigate.

This committee was chaired by Sir Walter Warboys and generally agreed with Spencer's findings. Which were that:

(a) Roadside signs are too small to be readily recognisable as such and to be easily read by drivers travelling at the normal speed of traffic;
(b) They do not have a simple, integrated appearance;
(c) The more important signs are not readily distinguishable from the less important at long range;
(d) They are often not effective at night;
(e) They are different from those used on the continent of Europe and only those who can read English can fully understand them;
(f) They are often mounted too high, particularly in rural areas;
(g) They are often badly sited in relation to junctions; and
(h) There is insufficient continuity of place names on directional signs.

– Worboys Committee, Traffic signs: report of the committee on traffic signs for all-purpose roads (1963)

The upshot was that British road sign design changed quite drastically mostly coming into line with the rest of Europe. The one downside of this was that the familiar black and white signs were to be phased out. As councils replaced signs, there were to be of the new style. Fortunately, the removal of the black and white signage (known these days as 'Pre-Warboys' signage) was not made compulsory and although some councils were more zealous than other in removing them, many survived, particularly fingerposts. My own county, North Yorkshire, luckily has many examples left standing; there is one in my own village. It was recognised in the early 2000s that these were worth keeping and a leaflet from the Department of Transport and English Heritage in 2005 advised that *'All surviving traditional fingerpost direction signs should be retained in-situ and maintained on a regular basis. They should be repainted every five years in traditional black and white livery. Other colours should be used only when these are known to have been in use before 1940'*. Again, North Yorkshire appears to be very good in sticking to this and hopefully they will remain for many years yet.

It is worth taking a quick look at the aforementioned Motor Car Act of 1903 which, while a fairly small act did set into motion a number of regulations that continue to this day and also started the ball rolling for the motoring organisation.

This old sign was found lurking in the undergrowth at the side of a dual carriageway. At one time the ring on top would have been red as a mandatory sign. ie you must turn left. Note that the sign itself has slipped down its pole. (CC)

Street Furniture, Alterations and other Interesting Things • 93

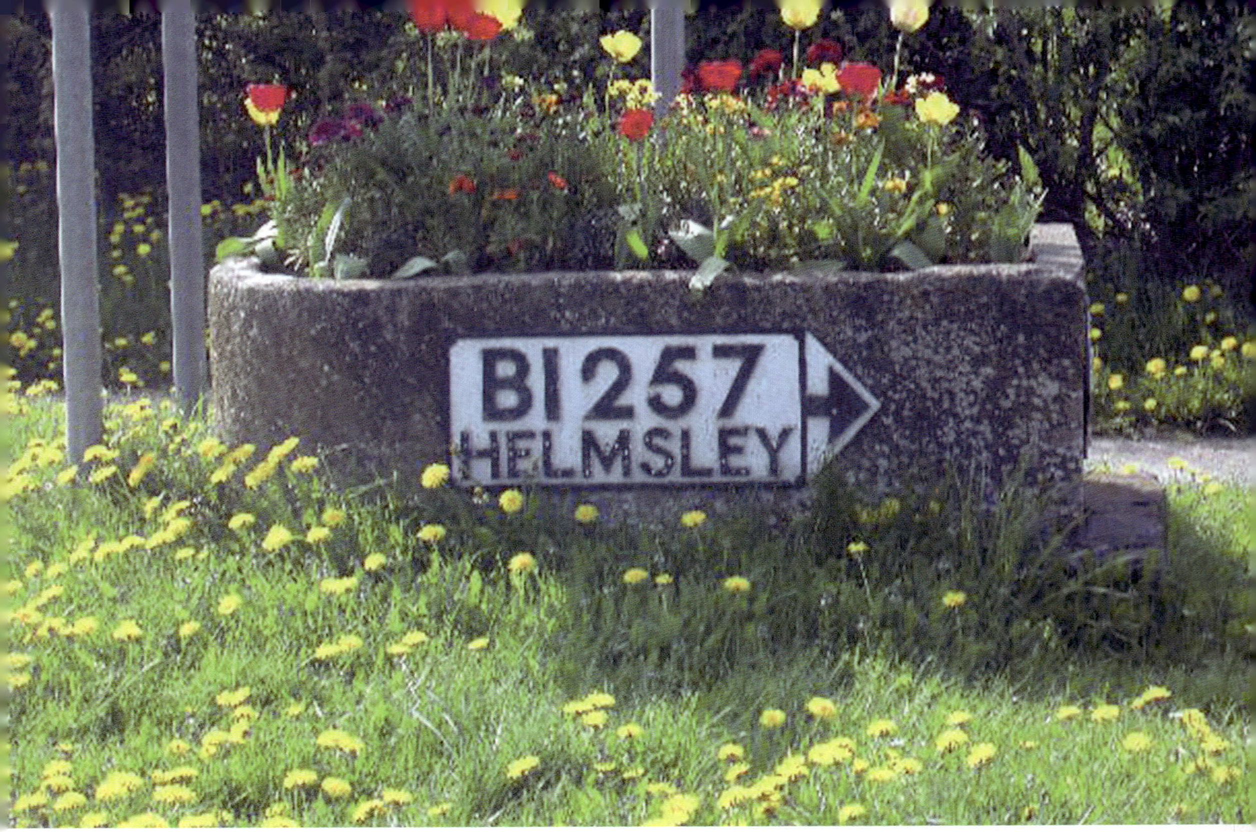
B1257
HELMSLEY

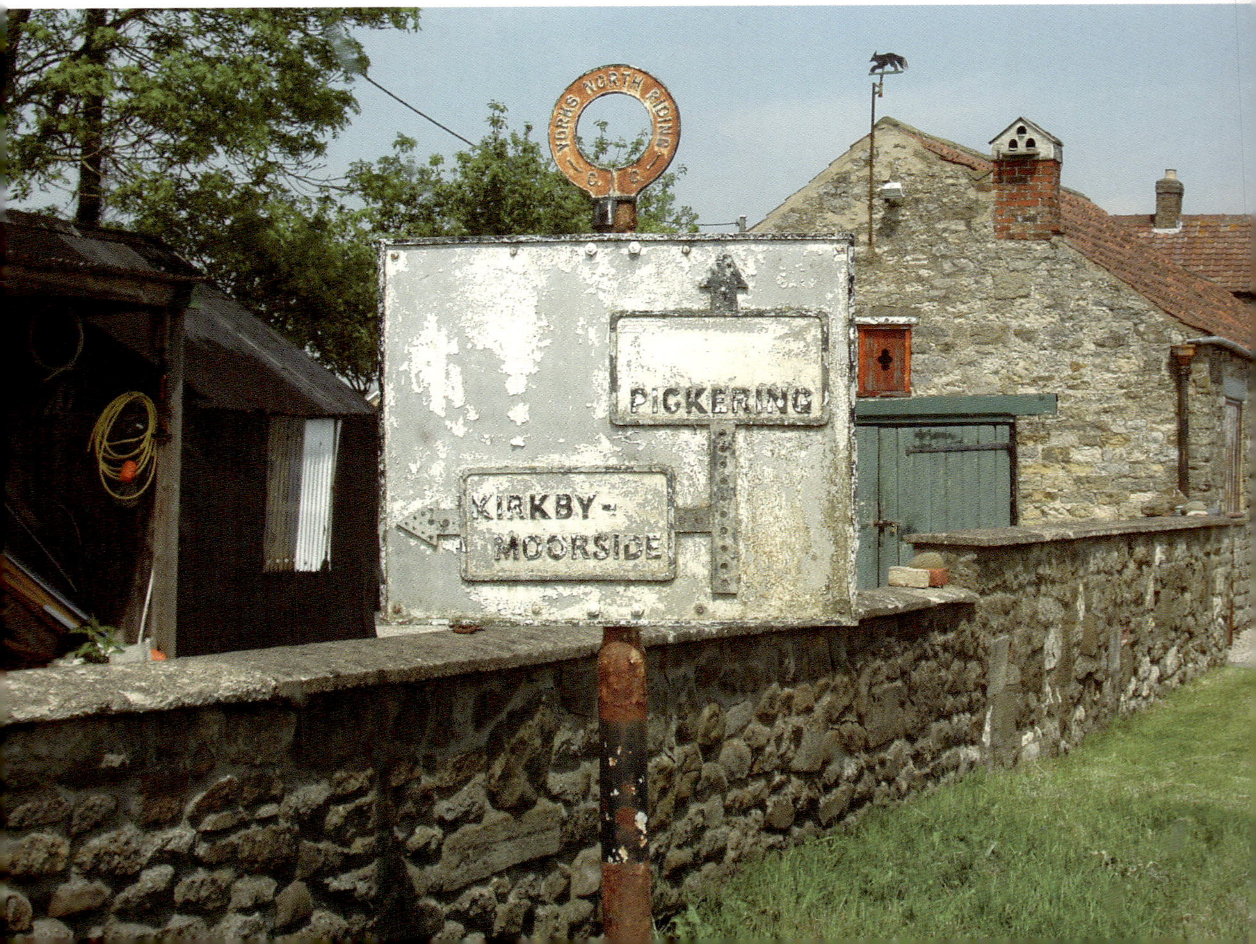
YORKS NORTH RIDING
C C
PICKERING
KIRKBY-
MOORSIDE

Other examples of Pre Worboys signage. (CC)

The Act had a number of sections including:

> Section 1 introducing the crime of reckless driving, and imposed penalties.
>
> Section 2 introducing the mandatory vehicle registration of all motor cars with the county council or county borough council in which the driver was resident. The council was to issue a unique number to each car, and prescribe the manner in which it was to be displayed on the vehicle. The Act also made it an offence to drive a motor car on a public road without displaying its registration number.
>
> Section 3 made it compulsory for drivers of motor cars in the United Kingdom to have a driving licence from 'the first day of January, nineteen hundred and four'. No test was required, the licence being issued by the council on payment of five shillings. The qualifying age for a car licence was 17 years and for a motor cycle, 14 years.
>
> The speed limit on public highway was raised to 20 mph from 14 mph which had been set by the Locomotives on Highways Act 1896.
>
> Section 9 allowed for lower speed limits to be implemented after a local inquiry.
>
> Regulations were introduced regarding the braking ability of vehicles.

It is quite revealing to read some of the debate in parliament concerning this act. Although it is too lengthy to include here, it is available to read in Hansard. Bearing in mind that this was 1903 there was clearly already a divided house as to whether the newfangled motorist was some kind of demon from hell or not! In no particular order all of these quotes come from that debate.

> 'It is not only the security of life and limb that has to be dealt with, but also the extraordinary discomfort suffered by people who live on the roads which motors largely frequent. Many houses alongside the public roads have been rendered almost uninhabitable, not only by the dust, which is an intolerable nuisance in the summer months, but by other inconveniences which follow from the improper use of this means of conveyance.'

'There can be no doubt that motorists are attempting to limit the right of the public with regard to the roads, and, as a matter of fact, motorists are in the position – I think it is an accurate definition – of statutory trespassers on the road.'

'Perhaps I speak a little feelingly on the matter, because in order to reach my home in the country I have to drive about a mile and a quarter along the Brighton Road, and everybody who has to travel along that road knows what an unmitigated curse and nuisance the motor may become when it is driven by a person hardly competent to drive, or who is careless of the safety or convenience of other users of the road. Along that road there is a constant stream of motors, and I have been practically compelled to give up the use of the road, and to forbid my children to ride along it.'

'As I have said before in this House, there is a great deal of difference between the danger of horse locomotion and motor locomotion. When you are driving a horse there are two brains at work – that of the horse and that of the man – and very often that of the horse is much the best, in the event of a difficulty. But with a motorcar there is only one brain. We hear a great deal about the development of road-side inns. I venture to say that a motorist who has been developing these road-side inns by taking a glass at several of these will be much more dangerous to the public than a man who has been doing the same thing, but is driving in a trap, and who will be taken care of by his steady old horse.'

'But the rash man may be a skilled engineer, and a man may perhaps be the finest driver in Europe and yet be wanting in consideration towards the other users of the road and the public generally. My experience is that in the worst cases of motor scorchers, or "road hogs," the men are nearly always very skilled, and their skill breeds a confidence that is dangerous.'

'A motor-car journal has very wisely been collecting the statistics of persons killed by horse vehicles; and the number killed or injured during a period of eight or nine months has been about 7,000.'

'Let us suppose that a police constable makes an arrest of one of those wealthy motorists whom he comes to the conclusion was driving at a dangerous rate. He brings the motorist before his Bench, and perhaps the Bench refuse to convict, and make strong remarks saying the case had no business to have been brought before them. Immediately an action would he started against the policeman – with the backing of the influential motor clubs – for false imprisonment, and the policeman would be threatened with all the terrors of the law. You would then have one poor policeman against all the wealth of the motoring fraternity. I think, under these circumstances, there would be very few police-constables who would see fit to arrest a motorist under the provisions of this clause. As a matter of fact, this clause would only be of use in two cases – when a policeman sees that the man in possession of a motor-car is obviously drunk, or when he has seen an accident. But that is like shutting the stable door when the steed has been stolen.'

Some interesting opinions there! Clearly being drunk in charge of a horse and cart was not a major transgression. Note the early use of the phrase road-hog too. And 7,000 people killed and injured by horses in less than a year!! Road deaths nothing new then.

However, it is the last quote which is very telling. Note the reference to the 'influential motor clubs'. Such clubs were started to give motorists such benefits as were provided by said clubs. The most well known in Britain are the AA (Est. 1905) and RAC (Est. 1897). Benefits of membership included early road signage much like the cycling clubs. The AA managed Britain's road signs until the standardisation act in 1933. Also, mechanical assistance and maps and guides. The other thing they did was to warn motorists of police speed traps. Clearly coming into the debate on the side of the motorist. This was the subject of a test case in 1910 where an AA patrolman was deemed to have obstructed an officer in the course of his duty. Both organisations have become companies in their own right in more recent years.

As we ride around the country, we see far more than road signs around us. We also see 'road furniture'. This term refers to all the rest of the items placed on our roads. It is worth taking a look at some of them. We will take them in historical order, but it is worth noting that many of these innovations were developed concurrently.

Obviously in the era of railways there were many places where roads and railways had to cross. Early on there was not much road traffic and it was simply expected to stop if a train was coming but as far back as 1839 gates at the crossings were made mandatory. These were simply field gates that were closed by a gatekeeper when a train was coming. The gatekeeper usually lived in an adjacent cottage. A friend of mine lives in one of those cottages on a disused line where coincidentally my late wife's grandfather was the gatekeeper many years since.

Over the years level crossings have become automated with various styles of barrier being tested. It remains an unsatisfactory method

The level crossing in my town mentioned in the text. The building in the background with the chimneys was a brewery. I remember standing on that bridge watching trains.

The same place today. The footbridge is gone as is the brewery. (CC)

of regulating road and rail traffic as both have become faster and more commonplace. Level crossings slow rail traffic down and cause holdups for road traffic. I can understand this as my local town has a level crossing in a very unfortunate place jammed right in between a river and a road junction with no alternative route. It closes about 4 times an hour and can cause dreadful congestion. This is the kind of thing that makes frustrated people try and get through after the lights have started which is a really bad idea. A derailed train can cause death and injury beyond the car passengers. For this reason, wherever possible level crossings are being phased out and replaced with bridges or tunnels. Unfortunately, our one is unlikely to get such treatment due to the proximity of the river on one side.

Another item that has been around longer than you might think is the traffic light. The first recorded traffic directing light was installed in London in 1868. It had semaphore arms and gas lights for use at night. It was 22 feet high and had a lever at its base so it could be turned to face the appropriate traffic by the controlling policeman. It did not last long though, apparently due to a gas leak it exploded a couple of months later!

Electric traffic lights were adapted around the US in the 1920s and in the UK in the 1930s. Like the level crossings, traffic lights quickly evolved gaining a third (amber) light and becoming automated and interconnected. The red, green and amber lights were used because this is what was already in use on the railway network.

Another clash on our roads highlighted by the 1903 discussion was that between road users and pedestrians. Obviously, pedestrians need to cross roads occasionally and although this was not a problem in the country, cities were already crowded in the time of horse and carriage, let alone in more recent times. Early pedestrian crossings were simply marked by an orange flashing light on either side of the road. They were called Belisha Beacons after the then minister of transport Leslie Hore-Belisha. The crossing was marked in the road by metal studs, the black and white stripes in the road were added at a later date and the zig zag lines much more recently in 1971. Many so-called Zebra crossings have been replaced with push button controlled crossings such as Pelican and Toucan crossings. These are traffic light controlled and do not have the orange beacons or zebra stripes being delineated by rows of metal studs across the road like early crossings. Old style zebra crossings do still exist and retain the Belisha Beacons.

Street lights in various forms have been around for a very long time. Over 2,000 years in fact, but the rows of lights as we know them with low power sodium lamps have been around since the early 1950s. They differ vastly in styles across the UK. More recently they are being upgraded to solar power and LEDs. I also vaguely remember seeing other posts in Birmingham when I was small. As tall as street lights but with a flared top. I was always told they were vents from the sewer system!

The other great help to the night time motorist was invented by a Yorkshireman, Percy Shaw in 1934. The Cats Eye. He put a pair of glass tubes with mirrors in one end into a rubber housing. This reflects the lights of a vehicle and when placed in a line clearly delineates the middle of a road. Cats eyes of different colours mark the edges of roads

A typical cats eye.

and junctions. These proved invaluable during the blackouts of WWII and were used extensively throughout the country during and after the war. They quickly spread worldwide and in 2006 were included in a top 10 innovations that Britain gave the world list.

The white lines and writing we see all over our roads is a fairly recent thing too. It was not until decent road surfaces came into being that the authorities were able to even attempt it. White dashes in the middle of the road appeared in around 1925 and the double unbroken no-overtaking lines in 1957 in London. It was the 1960s before crosshatching and wording became possible. Much more recently rumble bumps were added to the lines at the side of the road to warn an unwary driver that he was straying off the road.

A more unwelcome piece of furniture is the parking meter. Invented in the USA in the 1930s it quickly spread to cities worldwide and although subject to legal challenges over the years is still with us. Which brings us to the most hated piece of road furniture. The speed camera.

Some people seem to have always been against speed. While others have reveled in it. The constant argument has been raising its ugly head for many years. The first recorded law relating to speed in Britain was the Stage Carriage Act of 1832 which introduced the offence of 'endangering a passenger or person by furious driving'. Other Acts in the 1860s restricted the speed of steam powered vehicles to 10mph and then to only 2mph in towns and 4mph in rural villages. This Act included the infamous man with the red flag walking in front requirement. These draconian rules led directly to Britain lagging behind in vehicle research allowing the rest of Europe a head start. Their repeal and an upgrade to the speed limit to 14mph in 1896 was and still is celebrated by the London – Brighton Veteran car run.

More sensible speed limits have evolved over the intervening time; however, some councils still seem to great delight in slowing vehicles down as much as possible by creating urban assault courses of speed bumps, pinch points, chicanes and the speed camera. Reasons given usually include safety, fuel efficiency and environmental concerns. Speed cameras first appeared in London in 1992 but have been controversial ever since with many people seeing them simply as a revenue raising exercise as they do not always appear to be sited in places with an accident record, but places more likely to catch people out like downhill stretches of road.

On the other side of the argument are those who enjoy speed. In 1899 a man called James Gordon Bennett, a rich American newspaper magnate offered a Cup to the Automobile Club of France to be competed for by the teams of the National Motoring organizations of various countries. This was because France had already held automobile races in the 1890s on existing roads giving rise to the term road racing. The Gordon Bennett Cup morphed into the first Grand Prix in 1906 and is the root of modern-day Formula 1. That 1906 Grand Prix was run at the Circuit de la Sarthe at Le Mans. A circuit of closed existing roads. A number of drivers and spectators were killed in the early years and the road races were soon stopped and purpose-built circuits became the norm. The same could be said of motorcycle racing and such well known circuits as the Isle of Man TT and the North West 200 in Ireland lost their World Championship status over the concerns. The fact that these races are still run is due to what is known as Traditional Road Racing and a handful of circuits still exist mostly in Britain and a few places in Europe including one quite near where I sit. Oliver's Mount in Scarborough.

It could be said that many British bikers know of excellent

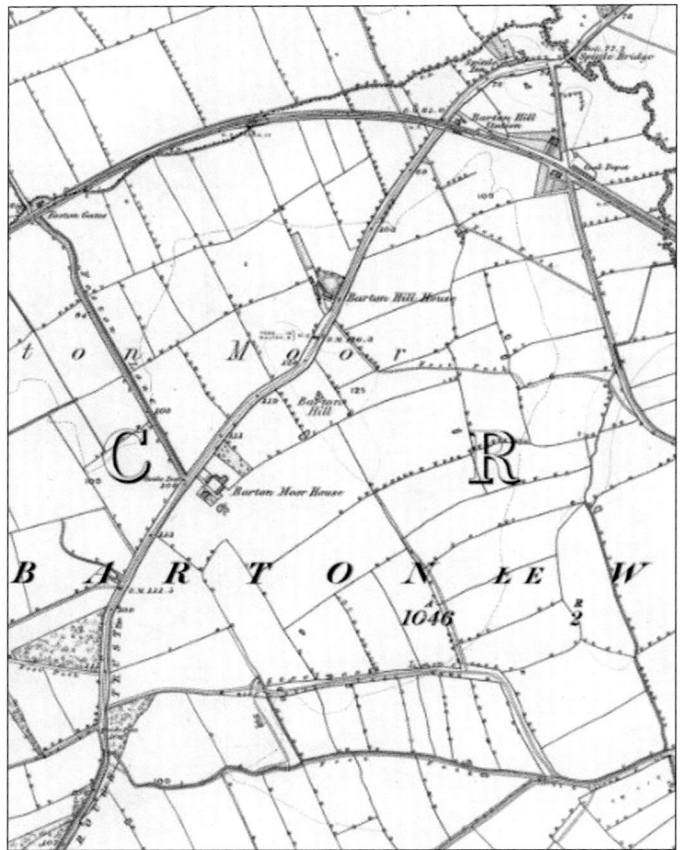

This old map snippet shows a stretch of the road from York to Malton.

'biking roads' and we all have our favourites. I live quite close to one end of what is known locally as the 'Helmsley TT', the B1257 between Helmsley and Stokesley in North Yorkshire. And an excellent biking road it is too! There are others across the country, the Cat and Fiddle run in Derbyshire/Cheshire, the A57 Snake Pass (Glossop-Sheffield) and the famous Hartside climb near Penrith in Cumbria to name a few. I am sure every area will have its favourites although we are blessed here with the Pennines, North York moors and Yorkshire Dales, Northumberland and the Lakes.

And finally, as roads are upgraded, what happens to the old bits? Well, some of them disappear for ever. However, all is not lost, we can still see bits of old road if we know what we are looking for. Often some things are simply not compatible with modern day traffic or are dangerous. Sharp bends which were not a problem for slow horse carriages are no good when it comes to much faster motor traffic. So, they are made less sharp, often leaving an ox-bow layby which was the original curve. Ox-bow laybys can be much bigger than a layby becoming stretches of old road in their own right. Sometimes drivable, sometimes not. As mentioned earlier, level crossings are being removed wherever possible, usually bypassed by a bridge leaving stubs of old road either side of the railway. The same can be said of old river bridges, sometimes too narrow for a modern road, they are also bypassed leaving them off to one side.

This overhead view shows the same stretch today. The A64 has been dualled and the old road is still visible as a cut off stretch off the main highway. This is known as an 'ox-bow' stretch. Sometimes they are left as laybys (ox-bow layby) (GEP)

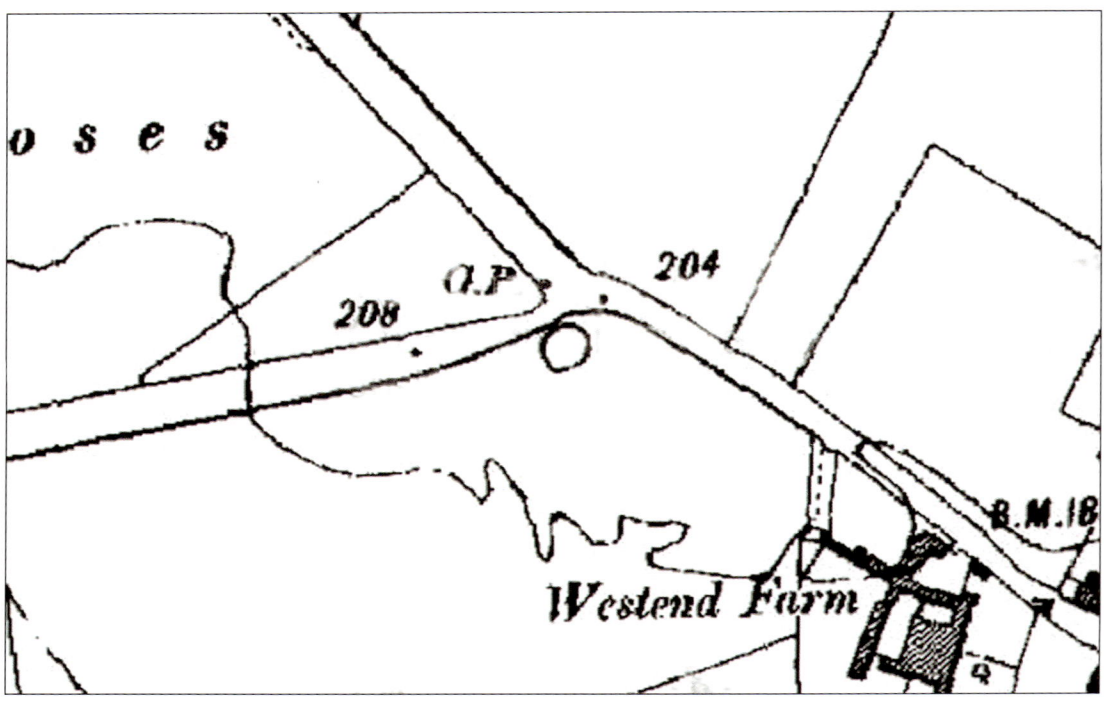

This old map snippet shows a fork in the road from York to Driffield.

When the larger road was upgraded (it became the A166), the side road was altered so that it met the main road at a T junction to make life easier for motorists coming along it. This leaves a characteristic triangular patch of grass where the road used to run. It's a dead giveaway. (GEP)

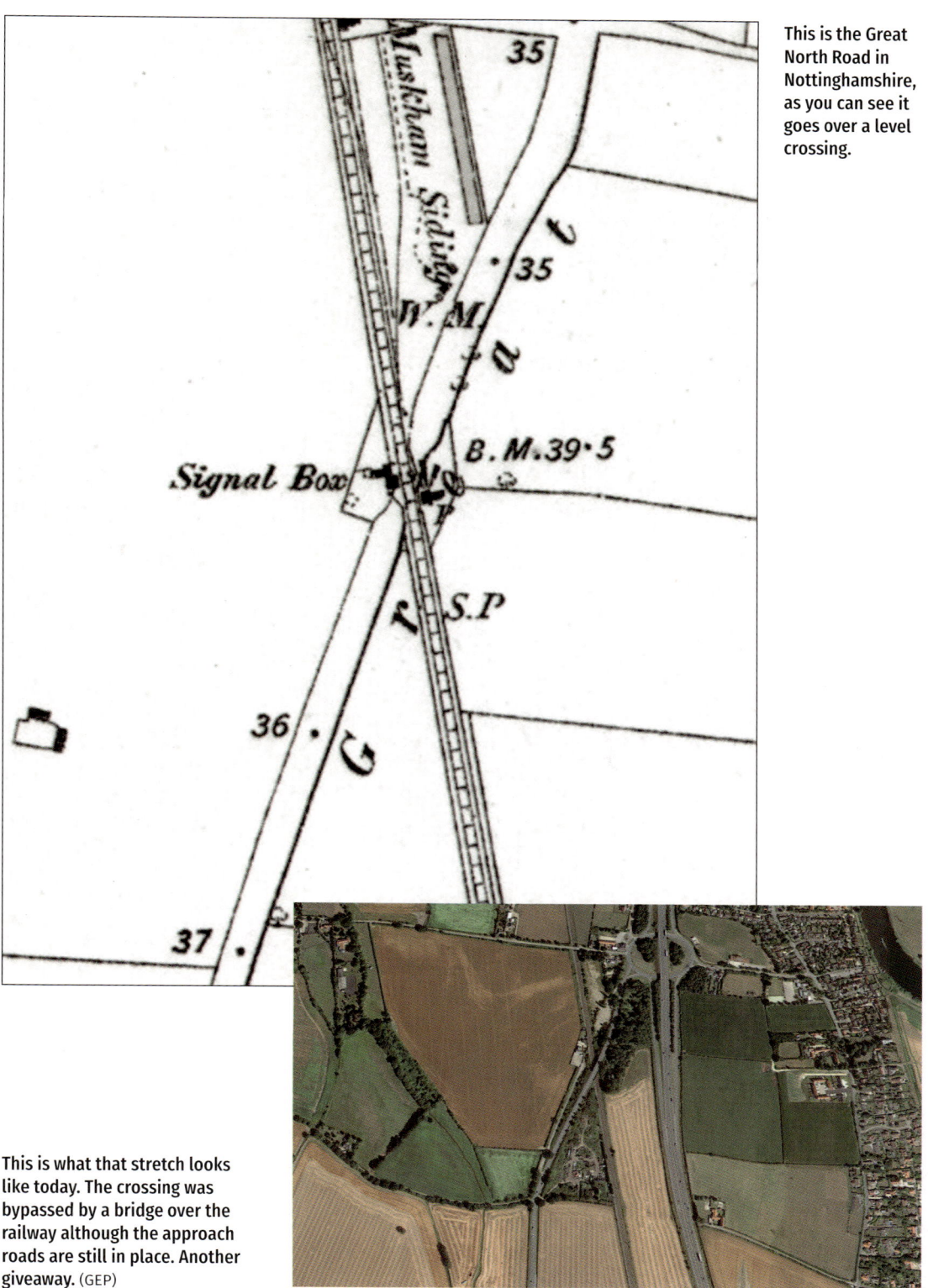

This is the Great North Road in Nottinghamshire, as you can see it goes over a level crossing.

This is what that stretch looks like today. The crossing was bypassed by a bridge over the railway although the approach roads are still in place. Another giveaway. (GEP)

Street Furniture, Alterations and other Interesting Things • 105

Also often removed are acute forks. These are made into proper T junctions leaving a tell-tale triangular patch of verge. Often where a new road has cut an old one in two there will be a dead end where there was not one before.

Another level crossing on the Great North Road in Sutton on Trent.

Also bypassed by a bridge. (GEP)

So go out and explore your area. Have a look at old maps and compare them with modern ones. This is easy to do on the internet these days. And if you find changes, go and see them and imagine what it used to look like.

Enjoy!
Wolfie – North Yorkshire 2024.

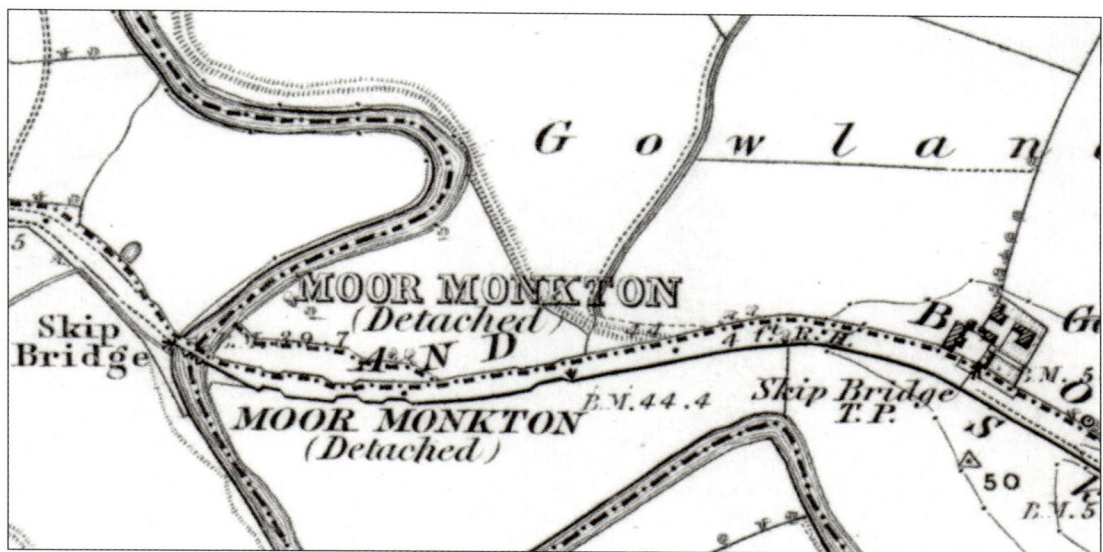

This old map shows a stretch of the York to Harrogate road where it crosses the river Nidd.

The road was upgraded and became the A59 and the whole stretch including the old bridge became a long ox-bow layby. (GEP)

This shows Healam (or Ealam) bridge in North Yorkshire on the Great North Road.

The modern overhead shot shows us an interesting picture. The bridge is still there sandwiched between two other roads. Interestingly there are 3 incarnations of the same road visible here. The old bridge was on the Great North Road. The road to the left was the southbound carriageway of the A1 dual carriageway, the northbound carriageway has been removed, its under the grass next to the southbound. And to the right we see the current A1(M). (GEP)

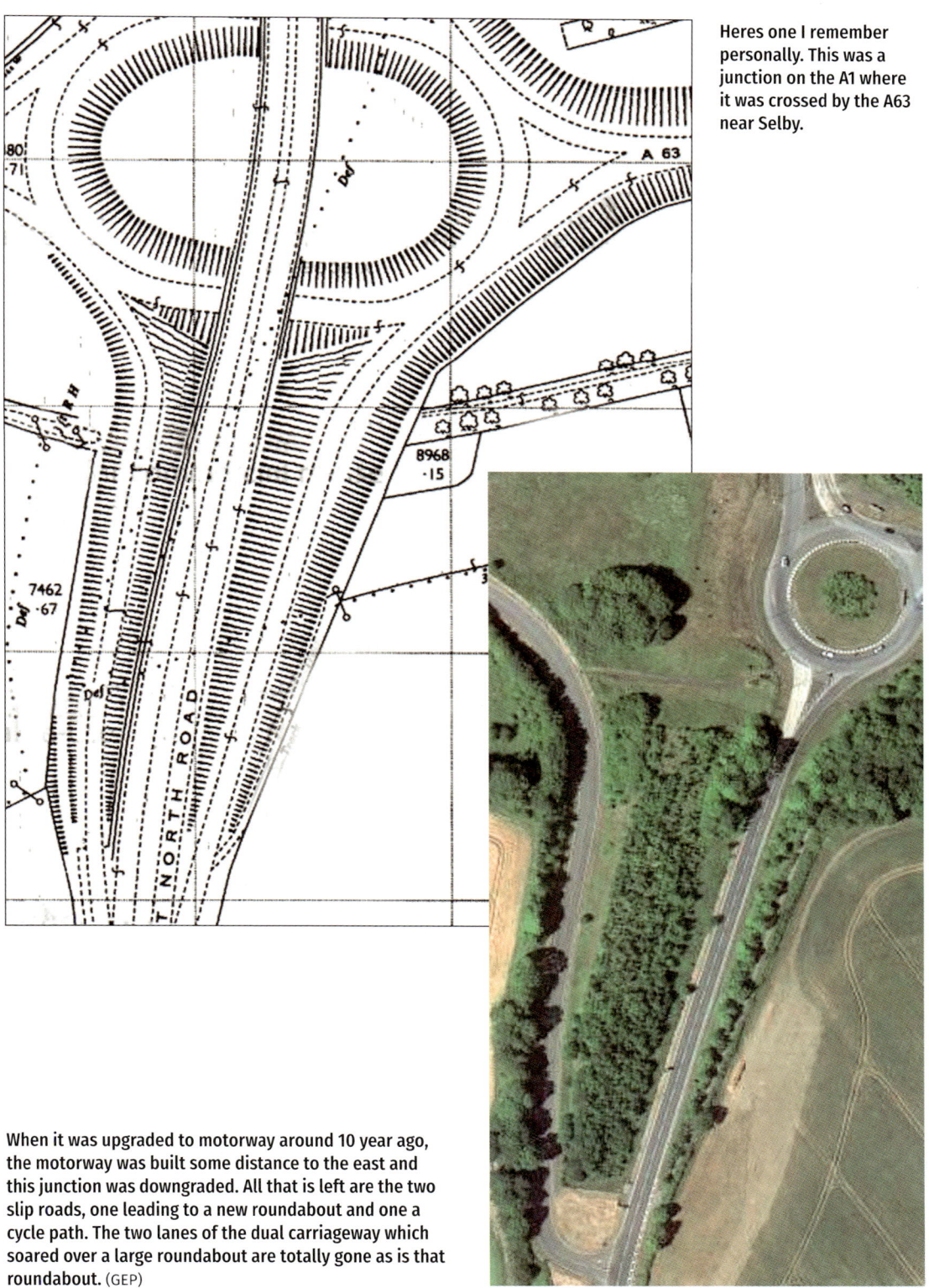

Heres one I remember personally. This was a junction on the A1 where it was crossed by the A63 near Selby.

When it was upgraded to motorway around 10 year ago, the motorway was built some distance to the east and this junction was downgraded. All that is left are the two slip roads, one leading to a new roundabout and one a cycle path. The two lanes of the dual carriageway which soared over a large roundabout are totally gone as is that roundabout. (GEP)

Street Furniture, Alterations and other Interesting Things • 109

This 1841 engraving by W H Bartlett shows a rather precarious road skirting Dover Castle.

The modern road is much larger although trees obscure the view. (GEP)

This view of a village street in Dosthill, Staffordshire shows a typically muddy scene.

Much changed today. (GEP)

Street Furniture, Alterations and other Interesting Things •

The Woodman Inn on the Great North Road as painted by James Pollard. Note the man looking back at London with the telescope. No chance of that now! This was once the main coaching inn on the exit to London on the Great North Road. The present building goes back to around 1810.